☆☆☆☆☆☆☆☆☆☆☆☆☆☆☆☆☆☆☆☆☆☆☆☆☆☆☆☆☆☆☆

"Come now, and let us reason together" is Lyndon Johnson's favorite quotation and his best characterization. I can't recall when I first heard him use these words from Isaiah. But for the thirty years I have known him—as a Congressional secretary, Congressman, Senate majority leader, Vice President, and now President—reasoning together, face to face, has been his method and his strength.

"It is essential in time of strife and turmoil to remind ourselves that progress *is* possible and our goals someday *will* be achieved," he tells us in this collection of some of our new President's public statements. And all who know him will testify to his extraordinary skill in getting things done—in achieving our goals—by persuasion, by reasoning together.

—*From the Introduction by Adlai E. Stevenson*

☆☆☆☆☆☆☆☆☆☆☆☆☆☆☆☆☆☆☆☆☆☆☆☆☆☆☆☆☆☆☆

A TIME FOR ACTION is an Atheneum Book published by Pocket Books, Inc.

☆☆☆☆☆☆☆☆☆☆☆☆☆☆☆☆☆☆☆☆☆☆☆☆☆☆☆☆☆☆☆

A TIME FOR ACTION

✩✩✩✩✩✩✩✩✩✩✩✩✩✩✩✩✩✩✩✩✩✩✩✩✩✩✩✩✩

A Selection from the Speeches
and Writings of

LYNDON B. JOHNSON
1953-64

✩✩✩✩✩✩✩✩✩✩✩✩✩✩✩✩✩✩✩✩✩✩✩✩✩✩✩✩✩

Introduction by Adlai E. Stevenson

Illustrated with photographs

An Atheneum Book published by
Pocket Books, Inc.

A TIME FOR ACTION

Atheneum edition published February, 1964

A *Giant Cardinal* edition

1st printing........February, 1964
4th printing..........April, 1964

"My Political Philosophy" appeared in *The Texas Quarterly*

This *Giant Cardinal*** edition includes every word contained in the
original, higher-priced edition. It is printed from brand-new
plates made from completely reset, clear, easy-to-read type.
Giant Cardinal editions are published by Pocket Books, Inc., and
are printed and distributed in the U.S.A. by Affiliated Publishers,
a division of Pocket Books, Inc., 630 Fifth Avenue, New York 20, N.Y.
*Trademark registered in the United States and other countries.
**Trademark of Pocket Books, Inc., 630 Fifth
Avenue, New York 20, N.Y., in the United States
and other countries.

L

CONTENTS

Contents

Speeches (*cont.*)

8 pages of photographs are inserted between
pages 96 and 97.

PUBLISHER'S NOTE

This selection from the speeches and writings of Lyndon B. Johnson was made, with his authorization, shortly after he became President of the United States. It is designed to be selective rather than complete and to present the principal expressions of his views in the high offices he has occupied since he became the Democratic leader in the Senate in 1953. All of the speeches and writings are given in full, as they were written and delivered.

These selections are arranged in chronological order except for the first one, which has been placed at the beginning because it makes a general statement of President Johnson's political philosophy and thus provides his own introduction. For subject references, the reader is directed to the index.

The selection and arrangement in this book were done by the publisher, who wishes to express particular thanks for assistance to Mr. George Reedy and Mrs. Dorothy Territo.

INTRODUCTION

"Come now, and let us reason together" is Lyndon Johnson's favorite quotation and his best characterization. I can't recall when I first heard him use these words from Isaiah. But for the thirty years I have known him—as a Congressional secretary, Congressman, Senate majority leader, Vice President, and now President—reasoning together, face to face, has been his method and his strength.

"It is essential in time of strife and turmoil to remind ourselves that progress *is* possible and our goals someday *will* be achieved," he tells us in this collection of some of our new President's public statements. And all who know him will testify to his extraordinary skill in getting things done—in achieving our goals—by persuasion—by reasoning together.

While these speeches reveal something of his views on the great public issues of recent times, they necessarily disclose little of his extraordinary managerial skill and political pragmatism. Lyndon Johnson is a master of the art of the possible in politics.

"Frequently in life I have had to settle for progress short of perfection," he writes. "I have done so because—despite cynics—I believe that half a loaf *is* better than none. But my acceptance has always been conditioned upon the premise that the half-loaf is a step toward the full loaf—and that if I go on working, the day of the full loaf will come."

President Johnson never stops working for his "full loaf." But he is more than a tireless, remorseless worker. He is a leader—a mature political leader —who knows that the role of a leader is to lead; to fall back if necessary, but always to lead and lead boldly, unafraid of the spears and arrows aimed at anyone who gets out in front in our political life.

One recalls the story of the French revolutionary who rushed to a window in the Tuileries exclaiming: "The mob is in the street and I must see which way they are going—for I am their leader." Mr. Johnson has not been at the window, but in the street—leading.

Like the man whose burdens he inherited, he doesn't like labels. "I am a free man, an American, a United States Senator, and a Democrat, in that order," he tells us in this book. Beyond that Lyndon Johnson does not wish to be pinned down. "The definitions of what I am," he says, "will have to be applied by others as they see fit." These speeches may help those who like definitions to make up their minds—though I suspect he would rather be judged by what he does than what he says. For Lyndon Johnson is first and foremost a man of action.

One sees this in his commitment to liberalism and to great humanitarian causes such as civil rights. Here I recall in particular his adroit and successful efforts as Senate majority leader to get our first meaningful civil rights bill enacted in 1957; and I would also commend to the attention of all these words he spoke at Gettysburg last Memorial Day:

One hundred years ago the slave was freed. One hundred years later the Negro remains in bondage to the color of his skin. The Negro today asks, "Justice." We do not answer him—we do not answer those who lie beneath this soil—when we reply to the Negro by asking, "Patience."

Lyndon Johnson knows the perils, the challenges, and the opportunities that confront us in this restless and perilous world of the sixties. As the President's representative he has seen Europe, Asia, and Africa at first hand. He has walked among the mighty and the meek, and talked to them in their palaces and villages. He knows, and is forever reminding us, that in too much of our planet, human degradation is still the rule and human dignity only a dream. And he knows that in this nuclear age there is no rational alternative to peace.

His commitment to the quest for peace was eloquently voiced in his speech to the United Nations in December, which is included in this volume. But it has many antecedents—as I remember only too well from the 1956 campaign, when to speak seriously of fallout, test bans, and nuclear disarmament was considered politically unwise. If one test of an effective statesman is to be a step ahead of his time, then Lyndon Johnson passed that test with honors in 1957 with the speech that you will find on page 28.

Like few political professionals I have known, our new President understands power—its uses, its sources, its limitations, and its corruptions. When Senator McCarthy, who did not, was finally censured by the Senate, it was Lyndon Johnson who made sure that every Democratic Senator present voted the right way. His colleagues on Capitol Hill will long remember him as a natural leader who likes a good fight, loves to win, loses with a smile, and, most important, knows how to win or lose and keep the respect of friend and foe alike.

The battles he waged and won for himself and for his party he will now be waging and winning for his country. The Presidential power he sought as a candidate came to him by accident in a dark and tragic moment of our history; and a few days later, facing a joint session of Congress, and speaking from his heart, he said: "All I have I would have given gladly not to be standing here today."

All he has—his vitality, his courage, his intelligence—he will now be giving, like all great Presidents, to the service of his country.

His style, people will say, will be different from John Kennedy's. Of course it will. But the drive, the convictions, the principles and programs that were a part of the New Frontier, will never be lost so long as Lyndon Johnson is President.

Knowing Lyndon Johnson, knowing his energy, his determination, and his goals, I also know that he will always be ahead of us, leading the way, pressing, persuading, and pulling us forward to those goals that he has long cherished—as a free man, as an American, as a United States Senator, and as a Democrat—and which he cherishes today as President of the United States.

ADLAI E. STEVENSON

MY POLITICAL
PHILOSOPHY

I am a free man, an American, a United States
Senator, and a Democrat, in that order.

I am also a liberal, a conservative, a Texan, a
taxpayer, a rancher, a businessman, a consumer, a
parent, a voter, and not as young as I used to be nor
as old as I expect to be——and I am all these things
in no fixed order.

I am unaware of any descriptive word in the second paragraph which qualifies, modifies, amends, or
is related by hyphenation to the terms listed in the
first paragraph. In consequence, I am not able——
nor even the least interested in trying——to define my
political philosophy by the choice of a one-word or
two-word label. This may be against the tide, but, if
so, the choice is deliberate.

At the heart of my own beliefs is a rebellion
against this very process of classifying, labeling, and
filing Americans under headings: regional, eco-

Reprinted by permission from *The Texas Quarterly*, Vol.
I, No. 4, Winter, 1958. Copyright © *The Texas Quarterly*.

nomic, occupational, religious, racial, or otherwise. I bridle at the very casualness with which we have come to ask each other, "What is your political philosophy?"

I resent the question most often not because I suspect it of guile and cunning, but for its innocence, the innocence that confuses dogma with philosophy and presumes that the answer can be given in a word or two. Our political philosophies, I have found, are the sum of our life's experience. God made no man so simple or his life so sterile that such experience can be summarized in an adjective. Yet we seem bent today on reducing every man's philosophy to a mere vital statistic, to the next question asked—of professors, students, public officials, job applicants, business executives, labor leaders, and many more— after age, weight, height, and color of eyes and hair.

Inquiries of men's philosophies do not fit this context.

It is a part of my own philosophy to regard individuality of political philosophy as a cornerstone of American freedom and, more specifically, as a right expressly implied in our nation's basic law and indispensable to the proper functioning of our system.

Our basic law—the Constitution—is distinctive among the basic law of all nations, even the free nations of the West, in that it prescribes no national dogma: economic, social, or religious.

Free enterprise, for example, is not mentioned. Nor are our parties or the party system. Nor is there any provision to require allegiance to any dogma or doctrine.

Yet government is an expression of philosophy, and active governments are inevitably guided by philosophers. As I see it, the mandate of our system —and, perhaps, the ultimate genius of it—is that the American people should be the true philosophers of the American government within the limits upon governmental powers set by our Constitution.

This is an ennobling concept, yet like many things noble and beautiful, it has certain frailties and we seem quick now to crush it. We crush out the individuality of our political beliefs and, by this process of high-speed sorting and classifying of Americans, automate our choice of courses and sterilize our explorations of the reasons why.

Some might suggest that my rebellion against this process is a show of the provincial Texan in me. I would disagree. Texans are independent and individual, but not the monopolists of these virtues that we sometimes suppose ourselves to be. The traits are American in origin and, fortunately for the Republic, are deposited quite widely, not part of certain regional hoards. Thus, I believe it is the American in me—even more than the Texan—that now reacts so strongly against the merging of the individual American into the mass in the name of dogma.

I realize, as I say this, that others might point to the Senate where I serve—and where I am, in fact, a designated leader of the majority party—and suggest that the example there of a two-party, two-philosophy system contradicts or is in conflict with this thesis. The opposite is so. Had I not been privileged to serve in Congress, I might never have come to hold the respect for individuality of philosophy that I do.

The very purpose of Congress, in our governmental form, is to arrive at national decisions by bringing together some 531 individuals, representing 170 million individuals, to achieve a consent on the way the nation should go. Were we bound by rigid dogmas, whatever their name, there would be no more cause for assembling Congress than for bringing the Soviet Presidium together. We are not so bound, and it is part—a great part—of my own philosophy that the Congress reaches a very dubious decision when its choices are made solely by head counts of the partisan division.

This leads to a listing of the tenets of my own

beliefs, the specific tenets of my own philosophy. I would set them down this way:

First, I believe every American has something to say and, under our system, a right to an audience.

Second, I believe there is always a national answer to each national problem, and, believing this, I do not believe that there are necessarily two sides to every question.

Third, I regard achievement of the full potential of our resources—physical, human, and otherwise—to be the highest purpose of governmental policies next to the protection of those rights we regard as inalienable.

Fourth, I regard waste as the continuing enemy of our society and the prevention of waste—waste of resources, waste of lives, or waste of opportunity—to be the most dynamic of the responsibilities of our government.

These tenets, I concede, are simple. They are certainly personal. For these are not tenets I have embraced or adopted, but, rather, beliefs I have—over fifty years—developed and come to follow from my own experience.

In the instance of the first listed, I realize that—in these times—the notion that each American has something to say and the right to an audience may seem excessively idealistic. I do not believe that is so, either in principle or in practice.

I am reminded always in my work at Washington of my own origins. I was born to the Hill Country of Texas, a remote region then, still remote today, although less so. My neighbors, friends, and relatives there live independently, self-contained if not self-sufficient.

They are distant from many national issues, yet neither their distance nor their limited information on any given subject makes them any less a party to the national decisions we reach in the halls of Congress. Knowing the folks at Johnson City and Blanco and Stonewall and Hye as I do, I know that it would be much more difficult for me to secure a unanimous agreement among them than among the Senators in Washington. Yet, in this individuality, my neighbors—or the constituency of all of Texas—are not different from Americans everywhere. There is likely to be merit in the views of the minority, quite as much as there is wisdom in the views of the majority. We have, as I see it, an obligation to seek out that merit, if it is there, and not merely to content ourselves with obliging the majority, for the majority's wisdom—however wise—is never the sum of all wisdom.

What we do, too often now, is oblige our patience with expedients. To grant audiences to 170 million Americans would be exhausting. So we make our divisions, our classifications, and our cross-classifications which permit us to forego the listening and the searching we ought to do. Trouble compounds when, having made our divisions on one basis, we extend the application to other issues and other decisions. Here we adopt in our American political philosophy the pattern not of philosophy, but of cults devoted to dogma, and we construct false equations which produce false answers.

This equation process is much a part of our party systems and contributes to the myth of the concept that "there are two sides to every question." True, there are two parties. That is not the same as two sides. But, by maintaining the two-side concept, we satisfy our consciences—again as a matter of convenience—that when a partisan majority has prevailed there is no need to examine either the majority's side or the minority's side again. Our reasoning is that since there are two sides, either side would have been acceptable, and hence the answer decided by political strength does not require closer scrutiny.

I think otherwise. This popular view is, I feel, very much counter to our American philosophy based on the thinking of men like Jefferson and Madison. I do not believe we have arrived at an answer until we have found the national answer, the answer all reasonable men can agree upon, and our work is not done until that answer is found—even if the process requires years of our lives.

Here fits the third tenet of my philosophy—and the fourth. Had America been bound by the Constitutional Convention to the philosophies of the eighteenth century—and by the limits of the wisdom and vision of those times—we would not have the nation that is ours today. Our rising greatness through more than 180 years has come from our freedom to apply our accumulating knowledge to the processes of our self-government. Or, to state it another way, this has come because America's course has been left to the living. Thus, the eighteenth-century philosophy of our Constitution has allowed for growth so that it is still strong, still good for our twentieth century.

Our nation, like all nations, is possessed of certain resources—resources of nature, resources of position, and resources of the human mind. Without conquest or aggrandizement, we cannot add to these basics. Thus whatever we are to be we must build from those things at our disposal, and to content ourselves with less than the ultimate potential is to deny our heritage and our duty.

Obviously, having come from a land like Texas, I feel this strongly. Of all endeavors on which I have worked in public life, I am proudest of the accomplishments in developing the Lower Colorado River during the 1930's and 1940's. It is not the damming of the stream or the harnessing of the floods in which I take pride, but, rather, in the ending of the waste of the region.

The region—so unproductive and insignificant in capacity in my youth—is now a vital part of the national economy and potential. More important, the wastage of human resources in the whole region has been reduced. New horizons have been opened for the fulfillment of young minds, if by nothing more than the advent of electricity into rural homes. Men and women have been released from the waste of drudgery and toil against the unyielding rock of the Texas hills. This is fulfillment of the true responsibility of government.

Conversely, the elimination of waste of this sort carries with it a continuing obligation for government—at all levels—not to create waste itself by extracting from the people the fruits of their new opportunities through improvident excesses in spending and taxing. This is an increasingly critical area for American government, but one to which we sometimes apply false standards.

Government can waste the people's resources by inertia, quite as much as by vigor. Government can, for example, fall into a state of complacency over the relative positions of strength between nations in the world. An international stalemate with communism would, I believe, be the greatest of waste of American resources and the resources of freedom, even though stalemate produced no war. A vital government cannot accept stalemate in any area— foreign or domestic. It must seek the national interest solution, vigorously and courageously and confidently.

These tenets are the tenets of my political philosophy.

Some who equate personal philosophies with popular dogma might inquire, endlessly, as to my "position" on this issue or that issue or some other. Philosophies, as I conceive them at least, are not made of answers to issues, but of approaches more enduring and encompassing than that. By these approaches I have set down, I can seek and, I believe, find answers to the issues of 1958 or 1978, as they arise.

By personal choice, I am a Democrat, for I can in that party best apply and express my beliefs.

As for being anything else, the definitions of what I am will have to be applied by others as they see fit, for I make no such distinctions myself.

I am, as I said in the beginning, a free man, an American, a United States Senator, and a Democrat, in that order, and there, for me, the classifying stops.

To the Senate
Democratic Conference
January 2, 1953

——————————————

My Democratic colleagues have accorded me the great honor of party floor leadership in the Eighty-third Congress. I accept the position in a spirit of gratitude for their generous support and with a prayerful hope that I can be worthy of their trust.

I believe that Democrats can all work together in harmony. One of my deepest convictions is that there are more vital issues to hold Democrats together than there are issues to divide them. We have had our differences in the past and we will have our differences in the future. I do not believe in suppressing those differences. Unity achieved by muffling dissenting voices is a cheap unity which serves neither our party nor our country.

My voting record is open to all. Regardless of whatever position I may hold in the Democratic party, I will not change the principles which have guided me in the past, nor will I ask any other man to change his principles.

There may be times when I will be in a minority

—not just in the Senate but among the Senate Democrats themselves. This I believe is unavoidable and would be unavoidable regardless of any selection that could be made by this conference. No man of integrity can live constantly in the majority.

We have all been sent here by our respective states and we all owe a primary allegiance to our constituents. Since this is a nation made up of states, I have never felt any conflict in loyalty between my state and my nation. I have represented Texas to the best of my ability in the past. I shall continue to do my utmost to safeguard the interests of my native state in the future, and I don't think there is another Senator who will disagree with that thought.

I respect and sympathize with the problems of all of my colleagues. I know they will be generous and extend the same understanding to me.

Wherever possible—and I sincerely believe this will be true in a majority of issues—I will seek to state the position of my colleagues as forcefully and ably as I can. In those instances where we may disagree, I will state and vote my disagreement. But I will do my utmost at the same time to protect the rights of those with whom I disagree.

We must frankly face the fact that the Democratic party, as well as the nation, is stepping out into new and untried courses. Twenty years of Democratic administrations have come to an end. New issues are arising and new issues will arise which we cannot foresee.

I have a great faith in the Democratic party. I am a Democrat out of conviction—not out of habit. I believe that the Democratic party is now—and always has been—the party that is best for America. I believe there are forces holding our party together greater than the issues over which we may squabble for the moment.

We are now in the minority. I have never agreed with the statement that it is "the business of the opposition to oppose." I do not believe that the American people have sent us here merely to obstruct.

I believe we are here to fight for a positive program—a program geared *not* just to opposing the majority, but to serving America. I think that is the real desire of every Democrat—even though we may disagree as to methods.

Working together, I think we can do more than merely preserve the gains of the past twenty years. I think we can go forward with a positive program —a program that is pro-American and not just anti-Republican. And if we go forward as positive Americans—and not negative oppositionists—I am convinced that the time is not too far distant when the Democratic party will again be in the majority.

THE OPEN CURTAIN

I am here tonight with a basic premise in my mind.

It is that you—the members of the United Jewish Appeal—are men and women who have dedicated your lives to helping your fellow man.

I do not assume this lightly—merely from the desire of a speaker to flatter his audience. It rests upon your enviable record.

I raise the point only as a predicate to the remarks which I plan to make tonight. This is the place and you are the people to whom I wish to define a new proposal.

THE WORLD WE LIVE IN

Never before in history have people been so badly in need of help. And the only kind of help that will serve today is the kind that the people supply for themselves.

There is no need to recite once more the realities of the modern world. We are all only too familiar with them—the cold war, the armaments race, atomic fallout, international misunderstanding.

Most of these factors have appeared before in history. There have been "cold wars." International misunderstanding has been a normal state of affairs for centuries. There is nothing new about an armaments race.

But for the first time, we now face the prospect of destroying ourselves—not as the *result* of an armaments race, but merely by indulging in the race.

THE ATOMIC RAIN

For several weeks our newspapers have carried daily headlines about the effects of atomic fallout. The scientists disagree as to the amount of damage that is being done to humanity by our nuclear test explosions.

But even the most conservative state flatly that there is "some risk."

I am no nuclear physicist. I do not pretend to have the scientific knowledge that would entitle me to pass judgment on genetics or the effects of Strontium 90.

But I do know that the experts are talking about

29

my children and your children. And it gives me no comfort to be told that some scientists think the risk to them is "slight."

NO MONOPOLY

It is even less comforting to assess the probable future of the armaments race even assuming that our children escape the fallout danger—whether slight or tremendous. If it continues, the future is bleak.

The intercontinental ballistic missile with a hydrogen warhead is just over the horizon. It is no longer just the disorderly dream of some science-fiction writer.

We must assume that our country will have no monopoly on this weapon. The Soviets have not matched our achievements in democracy and prosperity; but they have kept pace with us in building the tools of destruction.

With such weapons in a divided world, there will be little choice. We will return to the caves of our remote ancestors and burrow underground like the prairie dogs of west Texas.

REASONABLE ALTERNATIVES

There are reasonable alternatives to this unreasonable prospect. They are alternatives which are available to mankind—providing that mankind will adopt them.

Our present situation could have been avoided. Twelve years ago—when we had a monopoly on the atomic bomb—the United States offered to share the secrets of the atom with the entire world.

We asked in return only reasonable guarantees that the atom would never again be used in warfare. This offer had no parallel in history—and it would have converted the atom from an implement of death to an implement of life.

Two years later, this plan was approved by the General Assembly of the United Nations. It was blocked only by the Soviet Union and its satellites.

There is no point in reliving the past. I am not going to waste your time and my time in proving that the Soviets were wrong. Free people who have had access to the truth are already aware of the facts.

We live in the present. We no longer have a monopoly on atomic power. But there is a sound reason for recalling the events of 1946 and 1948. One aspect of those events may point the way to the future.

The Russian people have never had an opportunity to weigh the free world's proposal for the control of atomic energy. They were never informed about it openly and frankly. They never knew that Stalin provoked an arms race that, if continued, must end in the total elimination of mankind.

Today humanity is a great deal closer to self-destruction than it was ten years ago.

THE THREAT AND THE HOPE

And yet, because we are close to the threat, we may also be closer to hope. I do not foresee any quick Utopian solutions. A happy ending to the atomic-hydrogen menace will not be easily found.

But I am convinced, to borrow Churchill's phrase, that if we cannot see the beginning of the end, we can at least see the end of the beginning.

There are pathways of peace and progress open to all humanity. The statesmen of the world have one overriding duty—to help light those paths.

Where lie the signs of hope? They lie in the realm of reason.

THE CHALLENGE

The challenge is truly immediate. It involves actions that can and must be taken this year, now—during the remaining 206 days of 1957.

Our basic need goes by the technical name "disarmament." That long, rather dull-sounding word represents a host of complicated problems. The answer—even a beginning to the answer—represents the hope of all mankind.

We must initiate action on five objectives, each contributing to our crusade for disarmament:

1. Controlled reduction of military forces by all countries.

2. A start on a mutual, "open skies," foolproof inspection system.

3. A frank and open search for a method of suspending tests of the bigger nuclear weapons, under airtight conditions which give full protection against violations.

4. A reduction of everyone's stockpile of nuclear weapons and means for delivery under copper-riveted methods of mutual inspection.

5. And this is the key to ultimate hope: a world-wide agreement—backed by absolute safeguards—that no nation will make any new fissionable materials for weapons purposes—neither the three present nuclear powers nor those who may soon have the capacity.

LET THE PEOPLE JUDGE

How do we launch this program? We do so in the only way possible—in the only way that accords with American traditions.

We must create a new world policy. Not just of

"open skies"—but of open eyes, ears, and minds, for all peoples of the world.

I call for the "open curtain." Let truth flow through it freely. Let ideas cleanse evil just as fresh air cleanses the poisoned, stagnant mass of a long-closed cavern.

Mankind's only hope lies with men themselves. Let us insist that the case be submitted to the people of the world.

A few years ago this would have been utterly impractical. But great events have recently stirred the world. We must seize the hopes they suggest. We must not be blinded to those hopes by rigid reflections of the past.

Only four years ago the brutal Stalin died. Only a year ago the world learned that the new Russian leader, Khrushchev, had found it necessary to expose the depths of Stalin's evil. And only six days ago Khrushchev took advantage of America's facilities to come into our homes and state the communist case.

I am glad that he did so. I have complete trust and faith in our people.

They will not be contaminated by open communist propaganda.

We should welcome this example of direct argument.

But we must—I think—go much farther than this.

Let us take Khrushchev's technique and turn it back upon him. Let us use the program as the means to open the Iron Curtain.

As he has used our TV screens for his appeals, let us demand to use *his* screens for our appeal—the appeal of truth undefensive and undismayed.

We should ask Khrushchev to provide us with Soviet-wide uncensored radio and TV facilities. We should call on him to allow spokesmen of our own choosing to come into Russian homes and state our case—the American case—to the Russian people.

THE PATH OF PEACE

Once again we will place our feet on the path of constructive activity. We will look forward with joy rather than with dread to our children's future.

We live in a world where over two-thirds of the people are "ill-housed, ill-clad, ill-nourished." When the madness of the nuclear arms race is halted, mankind's creative efforts can be turned to their relief. We shall survive this century only if we find how to substitute human dignity for human degradation.

The people in this room tonight are dedicated to the cause of helping—rather than destroying—humanity. You have worked through the years to bring a measure of security and a measure of decency to your fellow humans.

LYNDON B. JOHNSON

SANCTUARY

You have been associated with many humanitarian causes—and one of them is creating a sanctuary for the oppressed. That sanctuary, Israel, stands today—permanent and enduring—in the midst of what was once desert.

Creating that sanctuary meant that rivers had to be dammed; fields had to be tilled; houses had to be built; the resources of nature had to be tapped.

These are the tasks to which all of humanity should be dedicated.

We have had enough of oppression and wars; of trouble and turmoil; of the frustration of every normal human impulse. We have seen noble impulses thwarted and turned to ignoble ends. We have watched the fruits of genius warped and turned into the paths of destruction.

This is not the work of the people of the world. It is the work of the small groups of selfish and twisted men who withhold from their fellow human beings the indispensable tool of freedom—the truth.

As you go about your humanitarian work, I want to leave you with one thought tonight.

You are people who seek to build, not to tear down. And when doors are opened so the people of the world can find the truth for themselves, we can all turn to building—building a better life for ourselves and our children.

The people can be trusted. It is time the case be turned over to them.

*To a Meeting of the
Democratic Conference
January 7, 1958*

———————————

I shall briefly summarize certain of the findings
which have been made thus far by the Senate Armed
Services Preparedness Subcommittee. Other members of the subcommittee will, in greater detail, deal
with specific areas of the investigations.

In all candor, however, I cannot begin these remarks with a simple recapitulation of the work we
have done. Illuminating as such might be, I realize
—as I know all members realize—that we have, thus
far, barely begun a work that will occupy and
dominate the Congresses of free men for lifetimes
to come. It is therefore of first importance that—no
matter how feeble our understanding—we strive to
establish perspective.

Our security may very well depend, above all else,
on how well and how quickly we grasp such perspective.

Let us begin with this fact: the ground beneath us
when we last met has been largely swept away. How

much is gone, how much remains, are questions no man can answer with authority.

The peril of the hour is obvious.

Less obvious, but of far greater importance, is the fact that beyond the peril lies a potential for peace that exceeds any ever before within man's reach.

Since August 30, when the first session of this Congress adjourned, the human race itself—without regard to flags or philosophy—has multiplied its capabilities to infinity.*

The exploitation of these capabilities by men of selfish purpose holds the awful threat of a world in subjugation.

The mastery of such capabilities by men wholly dedicated to freedom presents, instead, the prospect of a world at last liberated from tyranny, liberated in fact from the fear of war.

What this Congress does will at best be only a small beginning on what must ultimately be done— and will be done in decades and perhaps even centuries ahead. But, small as our effort may be in the long view of history, we can see that lack of sufficient effort on our part would be compounded throughout the ages ahead into a failure of tragic proportions.

We cannot, in the months of this session, assure

---

* On October 4, 1957, the first Sputnik was launched. (Ed.)

the nation's superiority: the era we have entered is too young, its ultimate dimensions too far beyond our vision, for us to anticipate so fruitful a result from our labors.

We can, however, by hesitation, by dissension, by narrow partisanship, do much to build an insurmountable barrier about ourselves and perpetuate our relative inferiority.

Responsible men have no choice.

We must work as though no other Congress would ever have an opportunity to meet this challenge, for, in fact, none will have an opportunity comparable.

We must, furthermore, bring to this opportunity a freshness, an originality, a diligence far exceeding our previous standards, for many of the concepts and ideas and rules which have applied to our actions in the past are no longer pertinent and applicable.

Let me expand this by dealing first with certain general facts which have been established in the short time of our hearings:

1. Our national potential exceeds our national performance.

2. Our science and technology has been, for some time, capable of many of the achievements displayed thus far by Soviet science.

3. That the Soviet achievements are tangible and

visible, while ours are not, is a result of policy decisions made within the governments of the respective nations. It is not—as yet, at least—the result of any great relative superiority of one nation's science over the other's.

The heart of the matter, then, is the national policy of each of the two great world powers, for this fact stands higher than all others: we could have had what the Soviets have in the way of technical achievements if it had been the aim of our government to employ our resources and capabilities in comparable pursuit of comparable goals.

From this, we deduce these matters of importance:

First, it is obvious that the Soviet valuation on the significance of control of outer space has exceeded that of our officials.

Second, it is equally obvious that our valuation has been based on factors other than the fullest realization of our scientific capability.

In essence, the Soviet has appraised control of space as a goal of such consequence that achievement of such control has been made a first aim of national policy. We, on the other hand, have—or so the evidence suggests—regarded other goals and aims as having a higher imperative.

Which nation is correct?

If our policy is correct in the approach that has

been taken, then the Soviet is ludicrously wrong, and some might dismiss the Sputniks as play-toys.

If the Soviet policy is correct in its approach, however, then we face the judgment that our own position may be tragic.

At root, this Congress must—before it does much else—decide which approach is correct. If the Soviet is wrong, then we would be wrong to undertake any sort of great acceleration solely to produce counterparts for the visible Soviet achievements. If the Soviet is correct, then we would again be wrong to limit our response to nothing more than a stride-for-stride matching of their progress.

From the evidence accumulated, we do know this: the evaluation of the importance of control of outer space made by us has not been based primarily on the judgment of men most qualified to make such an appraisal.

Our decisions, more often than not, have been made within the framework of the government's annual budget. This control has, again and again, appeared and reappeared as the prime limitation upon our scientific advancement.

Against this view, we now have on the record the appraisal of leaders in the field of science, respected men of unquestioned competence, whose valuation of what control of outer space means renders irrelevant the bookkeeping concerns of fiscal officers.

A Time for Action

The testimony of the scientists is this:

Control of space means control of the world, far more certainly, far more totally, than any control that has ever or could ever be achieved by weapons, or by troops of occupation.

From space, the masters of infinity would have the power to control the earth's weather, to cause drouth and flood, to change the tides and raise the levels of the sea, to divert the Gulf Stream and change temperate climates to frigid.

The meaning is, to my limited view, quite clear.

We have for many years been preoccupied with weapons.

We are even now concerned with what some currently regard as the ultimate weapon. But, when we perfect such a weapon for ourselves we may still be far behind.

The urgent race we are now in—or which we must enter—is not the race to perfect long-range ballistic missiles.

There is something more important than any ultimate weapon. That is the ultimate position—the position of total control over earth that lies somewhere out in space.

This is the future, the distant future, though not so distant as we may have thought. Whoever gains that ultimate position gains control, total control, over the earth, for purposes of tyranny or for the service of freedom.

Where do we stand now?

Let me summarize briefly the work of your committee.

Our staff has spent more than fifty days in intensive preparation for hearings which now have filled nearly 3,000 pages of transcript. Thirty-four witnesses have been heard before the committee. In addition, the staff has conducted 150 to 200 interviews with individuals concerned with the missile and satellite programs. Searching questionnaires have been sent to industrial organizations, leading scientists and engineers, and leading educators.

An effective, comprehensive, and important job has been done. Credit of the highest order is due each member of the subcommittee of both parties. Seldom have I seen men work with greater dedication; the debt due them is great. Likewise, the effectiveness and thoroughness of the committee's work is a direct result of the splendid direction afforded by our counsel, Mr. Edwin L. Weisl, and his partner, Cyrus R. Vance. Mr. Weisl and Mr. Vance are distinguished New York lawyers, members of the firm of Simpson, Thacher and Bartlett, and we are fortunate in securing their services.

From this committee effort, the essential findings developed thus far are these:

A Time for Action

The Sputniks now orbiting around the earth are not military weapons, but have a military potential.

Whatever their military potential may be, the present significance of these satellites is this:

First, the Soviet ability to put satellites of this size in orbit indicates a rocket ability far beyond any capacity we have developed; and, second, the satellites have gathered for the Soviet vital information about outer space which we do not have and which is decisive for any nation seeking to enter the space age.

Our primary effort to put a satellite into the skies ended in humiliating failure. It is my opinion that the humiliation could have been avoided: it was unfair to the dedicated scientists who are trying to do a difficult job and it reflected unnecessarily upon our scientific capabilities.

The people must have the truth, good or bad, but truth begins with perspective. It is not a proper perspective to reflect the responsibility for our lack of a satellite upon the men at work now in Florida. They are neither the source nor the cause of our failure.

Beyond the satellites, our committee has learned facts in open sessions about Soviet capabilities which are far more disturbing in relation to our present security.

First, the Soviets have almost as many army

divisions as all the nations of the free world combined, and a great proportion are highly mechanized.

Second, Soviet air strength is probably close to our own.

Third, Soviet submarines now number 500, while ours total 110, and there is evidence that they have some with missile capability.

Fourth, the Soviets are building 100 submarines annually, while we are building fewer than ten.

Fifth, there is no certain evidence of a Soviet nuclear submarine, but they have launched an atomic ice-breaker, and nuclear submarines, if not now in existence, will be soon.

In the field of the intercontinental and shorter-range missiles, the facts again are not comforting. The capacity to launch a one-half-ton satellite is interpreted by our scientists as evidence of the capacity to launch an ICBM against our cities. Other problems than the problem of propulsion are involved, however. We cannot fully appraise Soviet capacity in this regard. The safe assumption is that they have solved or will solve such problems as remain.

In part the answers that have been given to the committee are these:

1. Strengthen our strategic air force, about which Senator Symington will tell you more;

2. Accelerate and expand our research and development programs;

3. Speed up the development and manufacture of the intermediate and intercontinental missiles now being worked on;

4. Strengthen our educational system;

5. Provide a top-level, non-service-connected military planning staff for the Secretary of Defense;

6. Establish a new, advanced weapons development agency outside of the Defense Department to reduce the lead time in the production of new weapons—which, incidentally, according to evidence presented at the hearings, is over twice as long as the lead time required by the Russians;

7. Streamline the decision-making process;

8. Accelerate the nuclear submarine program;

9. Eliminate all overtime limitations;

10. Increase cooperation with our allies, particularly in the exchange of information;

11. Build shelters and store food and machinery as a precaution against Russian attack;

12. Build as quickly as possible an early warning radar system capable of detecting missiles;

13. Increase our interchange of scientific information between the free nations; and

14. Begin to do all of these things with a strong sense of immediacy and urgency.

The question in your minds, I am sure, is whether

or not there has been progress in actions taken during the past few weeks. I believe it is fair to say that some progress has been made since the inquiry began.

The President has named Dr. Killian as his personal scientific adviser. Also, the President has designated the Pentagon's special assistant on missiles as a "missile director," although in candor it must be said that it is difficult to define his powers.

The Secretary of Defense has been active:

1. He has removed the overtime restrictions;

2. He has restored research and development funds;

3. He has speeded up development and production schedules for missiles;

4. He has ordered both Jupiter and Thor into production;

5. He has reinstated a previously canceled launching pad for the Titan intercontinental missile;

6. He has established a new agency to develop advanced weapons;

7. He has ordered the Army into the satellite project.

These actions—as all, I am sure, will agree—constitute only a beginning of what eventually must be done. We can hope that the rate of acceleration will be adequate to the great challenge before us.

A Time for Action

Our problems have been listed. The suggestions about our future course have been listed. The actions taken have been listed. All of these relate to matters which are, essentially, military in character.

It is fundamental, I believe, that however urgent these military problems may be, we are faced with the unchanging problem of building a strong country, not a strong military force alone.

In this perspective, we cannot ignore the problems of three to four million unemployed workers.

We cannot ignore the grave problems of our farmers.

We cannot ignore the problems of our school children.

We cannot ignore the problem of housing.

We cannot ignore the problem of credit.

We cannot ignore the soft spots in our economy which are bringing some of our most vital industries into a difficult and troublesome climate.

We cannot ignore the growing problems of small business.

We cannot ignore the issue of conserving our natural resources.

These problems—and many more—must occupy our attention, and it becomes all the more imperative that we seek and reach answers of lasting durability for the road ahead.

One final question, the most important of all: Where do we go? What should be our goal?

If, out in space, there is the ultimate position—from which total control of the earth may be exercised—then our national goal and the goal of all free men must be to win and hold that position.

Obviously, attainment of that goal is no overnight thing. It may not come within our lifetime. Until it does, we must continue to have weapons—but we must recognize both their limits and their potentially short life.

With weapons, whatever their form, our ultimate gain is likely to be stalemate—such as we have had during the atomic age. But our position must remain flexible. We must forego a fixation on weapons as the ultimate of security. For, if we do not, we may build the space age's first—and last—Maginot Line.

Total security is perhaps possible now, for the first time in man's history. Total security—and, with it, total peace. This potential we must not underestimate.

Within the short weeks since October 4, man has become master of horizons far beyond our imagination. We must respect this mastery, and from that respect we must, more than ever, seek to bring all men together in cooperative effort. The goals now within reach of the human race are too great to be divided as spoils, too great for the world to waste its efforts in a blind race between competitive nations. The conference table is more important now than ever it has been, and we should welcome to its chairs all men of all nations.

To a Meeting of CBS Affiliates
Shoreham Hotel, Washington, D. C.
January 14, 1958

I am here here today to speak to a group which has a grave responsibility for informing our people.

In the chambers of the Senate of the United States, I am the designated leader of the majority party. That is a title of which I am proud but one which carries with it responsibilities that would cause any man to be humble. But it is a designation which, for this occasion, I have left behind.

I am not here as a Democrat.

I am not here as a leader of the Senate.

I am here as an American.

In this town we have the habit of dividing all things by lines of affiliation: the offices, the jobs, the various positions, and sometimes even our judgments.

At this hour in our history, I, for one, believe that there are certain facts which cannot be divided along such lines and certain judgments we must reach and decisions we must make together, as Americans, and as Americans only.

A Time for Action

Even as we sit here at these tables there orbits in the sky above us—around and around this earth—the most compelling fact of our times.

The Sputniks out in space have only one meaning.

There is no Democratic meaning.

There is no Republican meaning.

There is, in truth, no narrow American meaning.

In all history, mankind has never faced so great a challenge—or so great an opportunity. If outer space is allowed to become the province of the earth's imperialists, then the freedom we have fashioned at so high a price shall fall into eternal jeopardy.

If, however, free men set their sails for this new world as our forebears did when this continent was opened, then we have the opportunity of adding a new dimension to freedom—and with it, the very real prospect of reaching our goal of total peace.

These are exciting thoughts, exciting goals.

We would be out of character with our American heritage if we were not stirred by what we can now see on ahead in this new age.

We would be even more out of character—both as Americans and as free men—if we should lose this hour of opportunity in preoccupation with partisan thoughts of who is to receive the credit and who is to receive the blame.

Facts are not partisan, and the facts are these:

For a decade now, the free world—led by the United States—has summoned up its resources and resourcefulness to contain the most powerful and most ruthless aggressor ever to appear among the governments of the earth.

The physical containment has, in large part, succeeded.

It has succeeded, I should say, until now.

Today no responsible man can say or would say that continued success of our past policies is assured.

There is now abundant evidence that a pattern of history is repeating. We, like the dynasties of ancient China on down to the Republic of France, have built a wall against aggression, but now we find that we are the imprisoned.

The Soviet has, dramatically, leaped over our wall.

More importantly, we are awakened to the reality that advances of Soviet technology and science have made our wall of security a relic of another age.

Let me cite for you certain specifics, certain facts which all of us, as Americans, must sit down and consider together.

These are not facts of my invention. These are facts testified to by our military leadership coming before the Senate Preparedness Subcommittee, of which I am chairman.

First: The Soviet has under arms nearly as many divisions as do all the free nations combined.

Second: The Soviet air strength is probably close to that of our own.

Third: The Soviet submarine armada now numbers 500, while ours totals only 110.

Fourth: The Soviet shipyards are building 100 new submarines annually, while we are building fewer than ten.

Fifth: The Soviet capacity to launch a one-half-ton satellite into space indicates the capacity on their part to launch long-range ballistics missiles against our cities from Soviet soil.

Sixth: The Soviet has now the capacity to launch, from land bases or from its submarines, shorter-range missiles against our installations at home and overseas.

These are military facts. They are important. I would mislead you if I did not say that there are more, more which in time I believe should become public knowledge.

What is the sum of these facts?

The facts of comparative strength between the two strong powers do not add up to disaster—but they do, clearly, total up to peril.

For the moment, the stalemate is not clearly broken. The Soviet striking power is great and growing greater, but our retaliatory power is great, also. This the Soviet knows, as we know.

The Soviet, however, also knows—as we must come to know—that the rate of growth of their striking power far exceeds ours.

We are behind but we are not yet hopelessly behind. Our peril becomes a disaster when we fall so far behind that there is no hope of recovery. It is to the prevention of that disaster all free men must now dedicate their efforts.

How is such disaster to be prevented?

Some, looking back to the past, will answer only that the nation must retool its productive capacity, get ready for a massive effort, and move forward to match the Soviet Sputnik-for-Sputnik, missile-for-missile, sub-for-sub.

If war were inevitable, I would join in such a call.

But no man who looks beyond the moment will suggest that war is the inevitable consequence of mankind's new adventure into space. I, myself, am confident that it is not.

Space may well be the sea in which the human race will someday find an island of peace.

To reach that island, we need more than weapons.

We need, in fact, to free ourselves of the bonds of a weapon psychology.

Our greatest need in this hour is to unleash the pioneering spirit and the daring and brilliance of our people and set this nation's course on the pursuit of peace.

We cannot, of course, ignore the need for weapons now.

We need a faster rate of production for our missiles, far faster than any yet permitted or any yet envisioned.

We need continued production of our proved long-range bombers for our Strategic Air Command.

We need an acceleration of our submarine production.

We need these things now, for this reason:

In the past we have had the time to mobilize and build our strength while others fought—on their soil—the wars we were eventually to enter and help provide the margin of victory.

We shall not have such time again.

Our own soil is within the target range of a hostile nation for the first time in the American experience.

For the next ten years or more, we must be ready every night for any challenge that might come before morning. There is no other way.

Behind the security that such strength affords, though, we must do more than content ourselves with a stalemate. We must lay aside the illusion that a nation is strong merely because its military strength equals that of its adversaries.

If we can now buy time, and I believe that we can, we must make certain that we make proper use of what we purchase.

This means, as I see it, that we must change our ways—and those changes will make this both a happier land and a better world.

We have had since the end of World War II much time.

The evidence is indisputable that we have not used that time to full advantage.

What has been wrong? Why have we lagged?

Why do we stand now in a posture of relative weakness?

When such a question is asked, as it should be asked, there is an ever-present danger that we shall frame our answers in terms of credit and blame.

To do this now could well be fatal.

There is little question that wrong decisions have been made.

These errors are not divided along any partisan lines.

Furthermore, there is little doubt that such decisions, picked out of the context of the past, may seem glaringly wrong today, but at the time many of them met with majority approval.

As Prime Minister Churchill told the House of Commons on June 18, 1940: "If we open a quarrel between the past and the present, we shall find that we have lost the future." I say that such must be our creed at this hour.

It is with that creed before us that we must proceed, as responsible men, to assess the position of free men in the world today.

I see no gain in picking petty quarrels with the past.

I myself am willing to draw a line at the here and now, and measure responsibility in terms of what is done for the future rather than in terms of what was done in the past.

From this base, I believe we can take a more honest look at the problems we face.

What are those problems? Let me call them as I see them.

First and foremost, I believe that we are paying too high a price for conformity.

Ours has been, always, a nation built by the greatness of men's hearts and spirits and minds. America's vigor has come from the originality, the freshness, the vision of our people—all our people, not merely an intellectual élite.

For a decade now, we have seen growing a climate of contempt for these values. We are paying a price for that.

Our investigating committee has found, in some most striking examples, that this has been at the heart of some of our preparedness difficulties.

The fight to build for this nation an atomic submarine is a record of the persistence against great odds of one man, Admiral Rickover, who believed that it could be built. Because he was more determined to perform than to conform, this brilliant man was—on numerous occasions—shunted into obscurity and his services to the nation were very nearly lost.

This past few days, in our committee room, I sat two feet away from a great Army general and watched him choke back the tears of deep emotion. He told us that his decision to retire from service was final. He said he could not speak freely and he could not support a policy which meant placing American troops in the range of enemy missiles without adequate weapons of defense.

Over and over again, I have heard—and our committee has heard—the leading military men of this nation come before us and say that a conventional system has cut back on our programs for unconventional developments.

Over and over, we have heard them say that we are not, even yet, doing all that we could and should be doing to move forward in this hour of challenge.

This is not the road to strength.

This is not the road America should travel.

We must turn to the dedicated men of vision and

welcome them into the councils of respect and dignity.

We must provide a climate in which the men and women of our universities, our research centers, our career services, our world of journalism and communications, can make a full contribution of their talents.

Let me make this point clear.

It is not true that the abilities of Soviet science far exceed those of our American scientists.

As free men, who respect the freedom of man's mind, we must not allow political policies to chain our most priceless resource.

As we face this problem of removing the fetters from our capacity, we must also remove the fetters of tradition from our policy.

Our defensive strategies, in a military sense, are undergoing reappraisal and re-examination.

It would be a mistake to stop there.

Our foreign policies require the same reappraisal.

So, also, do our domestic policies and values.

We have, for long, held a position of strength in world affairs. That position is no longer secure. We must not be so inflexible that we can imagine no changed policy to cope with a changed position.

Domestically, likewise, each of you as businessmen know that our economy is now undergoing a period of change. This change is not merely a cycle through which we are passing. There are new problems, new challenges arising to the very functioning of our system.

Channels of distribution are undergoing change. Changes are evident in consumer demand and consumer taste.

Profoundly important population shifts are continuing.

We must not wait for calamity before undertaking a cure.

Just as we erred in our estimate of what Soviet gains might mean in the realm of technology, so can we err by complacency in our estimate of what domestic losses might mean in the realm of our economic health.

These things I mention only briefly, to emphasize that in this challenging period we need more, far more, than a purely military response to the Soviet challenge.

We need the marshaling of our resources, physical and mental, such as we have never had before.

We need imagination and freshness.

We need force and boldness in our leadership.

We need, further, I believe, to look beyond the danger evident now to see the horizons of peace in outer space.

I am no scientist and I do not pretend to be.

But the brilliant men of this age—the brilliant

minds of America—tell us things that we cannot ignore.

Out in space, there is the power to control the earth's weather, to change the climate where we live, to alter the tides and direct the Gulf Stream on a different course.

From space, snapshots can be taken of your backyard.

The whole technology of communication can be changed.

It is a fascinating, daring, exciting world.

The frontier it opens for human advancement exceeds any man has ever faced.

Surely we cannot, as leaders of free men, ignore it.

Surely we cannot, with this opportunity before us, fail to see that this affords us the one clear course to recapture the initiative for freedom.

Here is an opportunity to bring men together in common cause as never before.

Here is an opportunity for us to sponsor the flourishing of mankind's genius.

Before this session of Congress ends, I am hopeful that we shall be able to establish in our government a proper agency for direction of a new national effort in this realm.

I am hopeful, also, that we shall be able to provide a program for the enlargement of our research activities, making the laboratories and the equipment available to draw the best from the minds of our people.

I am hopeful that, furthermore, we shall be able to foster the strengthening of our total educational process, not to produce an army of technicians, but, rather, to pour forth legions of broadly-educated men and women.

As we do these things, I trust that in our relations with other nations we shall be imaginative, and that we shall make it evident that America's free-world leadership is not sterile.

We should certainly make provisions for inviting together the scientists of other nations to work in concert on projects to extend the frontiers of man and to find solutions to the troubles of this earth.

Our President, holding as he does the esteem of men throughout the world, has a rare opportunity to lead in this labor boldly and forcefully, and in the vigorous pursuit of peace he will find the nation undivided in his support.

Further, it would be appropriate and fitting for our nation to demonstrate its initiative before the United Nations by inviting all member nations to join in this adventure into outer space together.

The dimensions of space dwarf our national differences on earth.

A Time for Action

If we are to win space as the outpost of peace, all men may—and should—share in that endeavor.

We, with our great resources and our great abilities, must not allow the leadership to slip from our grasp.

The world in which we live is a world in which danger abounds.

There is no greater danger, though, than for us to shrink from the responsibilities of the hour.

Ahead, if we move with speed, if we move with daring, we shall find fulfillment of our quest for peace.

If we are to reach such a goal, our response must begin now. This, more than we realize, is the year of decision, the year our course is set.

In such a year, we need be responsible men, loyal to our nation, faithful to freedom, strangers to partisanship, and friends with the imagination that has been so much a part of our heritage.

*To the First Committee
on Outer Space
United Nations, New York
November 17, 1958*

———————————

I come today with one purpose.

I am here to express to you the essential unity of the American people in their support of the goals of the resolution offered now in their name.

This resolution is presented, as our system requires, by the representative of the executive branch of our government. I speak here today at its request.

The executive position in the United States is held by the Republican party through the mandate of the people.

I am here as a member of one house of the legislative branch in which the majority position is held —also at the mandate of the people—by the Democratic party, of which I am a member.

These are distinctions.

They are not—on this resolution—differences.

On the goal of dedicating outer space to peaceful purposes for the benefit of all mankind, there are no differences within our government, between our parties, or among our people.

The executive and the legislative branches of our government are together. United we stand.

There need be no differences among us here.

The very opportunity of the issue before this Assembly is to erase the accumulated differences of our earth's long and troubled history and to write across the vastness of space a proud new chapter of unity and peace.

Men have not faced such a moment of opportunity before.

Until now, our strivings toward peace have been heavily burdened by legacies of distrust and fear and ignorance and injury.

Those legacies do not exist in space.

They will not appear there unless we send them on ahead.

To keep space as man has found it, and to harvest the yield of peace which it promises, we of the United States see one course—and only one—which the nations of earth may intelligently pursue. That is the course of full and complete and immediate cooperation to make the exploration of outer space a joint adventure.

There is, I emphasize, no other course.

In saying this, I express no personal belief alone —but rather, I convey to you the conviction of my countrymen and the force of the American decision which has already been established.

The American people—through their elected representatives in the Congress—have spoken their aims and their purposes. The will of the people is now fixed in our laws and our policies.

The end is peace.

The means to that end is international cooperation.

This is—and this will remain—the American decision.

Eleven months ago, the Senate Preparedness Subcommittee submitted to the full Senate a report on an exhaustive inquiry into the satellite and missile program of the United States. In that report, the bipartisan membership of the subcommittee made this unanimous declaration:

> The immediate objective is to defend ourselves, but the equally important objective is to reach the hearts and minds of men everywhere so that the day will come when the ballistic missile will be merely a dusty relic in the museums of mankind and men everywhere will work together in understanding.

On July 29 of this year, the Congress in an act signed by the President established in the executive branch an agency under civilian control to guide and direct our national efforts in the exploration of space. By the act creating this agency, Congress embedded in the permanent law of the United States the following declaration of policy:

> The Congress hereby declares that it is the policy of the United States that activities in space should be devoted to peaceful purposes for the benefit of all mankind.

Further, in the same section of that act, Congress stated as a firm objective of the national effort the following:

> Cooperation by the United States with other nations and groups of nations in work done pursuant to this act and in the peaceful application of the results thereof.

Subsequent to that, the majority leader of the House of Representatives, the Honorable John McCormack, introduced before that body a resolution expressly requesting the President of the United States to submit to the United Nations the question of international cooperation in dedicating outer space to peaceful purposes only.

That resolution received the earnest support of the

full membership of the Foreign Affairs Committee of the House and it was adopted unanimously by the full membership of the House of Representatives.

In the Senate, the Foreign Relations Committee under the chairmanship of the Honorable Theodore Green likewise accorded to the resolution the most serious study and recommended without dissent that it be adopted. The Senate of the United States—like the House of Representatives—gave to the resolution the unanimous support of the Senators of both parties. Thus, it is a matter of record that the sense of the full membership of the Congress of the United States is that this question should be here on the agenda of the nations of the world. It is also the Congressional view that this organization should assume the responsibility of leadership in promoting international cooperation in the exploration of outer space.

This is the American decision, expressed firmly in the resolutions of policy by the elected representatives of the people and established solidly by them in the cornerstone law of our nation's space effort.

The resolution before this Assembly now embodies fully the will of the Congress and the will of the people whom the members of the Congress serve.

Thus I can—and I do—commend it to you for adoption. The record already made assures you the continuing support of the Congress for the cooperative endeavors toward peaceful uses of outer space which the resolution contemplates.

The full dimensions of the promise of space are now beyond the scope of our knowledge and our imagination. To presume that we have more now than merely a glimpse of those dimensions would be both a vain and, perhaps ultimately, a fatally limiting error.

At this moment, the nations of the earth are explorers in space, not colonizers. Hence, it is proper that this Assembly should provide—first—the means for the United Nations to encourage and inspire that exploration.

That is contemplated in the form of this resolution, which would create an exploratory *ad hoc* committee of representatives of member nations to carry out the following tasks:

First, to inventory the activities and resources of the United Nations, its specialized agencies, and other international bodies relating to peaceful uses of outer space;

Second, to determine areas of international cooperation and programs which could be undertaken under the auspices of this organization by member nations without regard to their present stage of economic or scientific advancement;

Third, to consider the future form of internal

71

organization in the United Nations which would best facilitate full international cooperation in this field; and

Fourth, to survey the nature of the legal problems which may arise in implementation of this joint adventure among the nations of the earth.

These are essential first steps. Until these explorations are conducted, orderly procedure to the broader horizons beyond will not be possible. Thus, to impede this first step is to impede all progress toward the goals of peace which men of faith believe exist in the realms of space.

While these are first steps, they are decisive steps and we cannot be unmindful of the precedents which, if established now, may influence or even control the longer steps ahead.

We of the United States have recognized and do recognize, as must all men, that the penetration into outer space is the concern of all mankind. All nations and all men—without regard to their roles on earth—are affected alike by what is accomplished over their heads in outer space.

If nations proceed unilaterally, then their penetrations into space become only extensions of their national policies on earth. What their policies on earth inspire—whether trust or fear—so their accomplishments in outer space will inspire also.

For nations given to aggression and war and

tyranny on earth, unilateral success in space technology would only multiply many times over their threat to peace.

Thus, it is to the interest of nations dedicated to peace and freedom that the opportunity of space not be perverted to the end of aggression and control over earth by the aggressors.

Recognizing this as true, men of peace will recognize fully the necessity to proceed without delay on the first step which is here proposed.

Today outer space is free. It is unscarred by conflict. No nation holds a concession there.

It must remain this way.

We of the United States do not acknowledge that there are landlords of outer space who can presume to bargain with the nations of the earth on the price of access to this new domain.

We must not—and need not—corrupt this great opportunity by bringing to it the very antagonisms which we may, by courage, overcome and leave behind forever through a joint adventure into this new realm.

What man has done thus far has been the result directly of international cooperation on an informal basis by men of science through the years.

The success, further, of the formal cooperation undertaken in observance of the International Geophysical Year foretells the high promise offered by enlargement of our goals and intensification of our support and efforts.

We know the gains of cooperation. We know the losses of failure to cooperate.

If we fail now to apply the lessons we have learned, or even if we delay their application, we know that the advances into space may only mean adding a new dimension to warfare.

If, however, we proceed along the orderly course of full cooperation, we shall by the very fact of cooperation make the most substantial contribution yet made toward perfecting peace.

Men who have worked together to reach the stars are not likely to descend together into the depths of war and desolation.

It is the American vision, I believe, that out of this fresh start for humankind which space affords, man may at last free himself of the waste of guarding himself against his ignorance of his neighbors.

Barriers between us will fall as our sights rise to space.

Secrecy will cease to be. Man will come to understand his fellow man—and himself—as he has never been able to do. In the infinity of the space adventure, man can find growing richness of mind, of spirit, and of liberty.

The promise of this moment of opportunity is great.

We of the United States believe that this Assembly will honor the moment and fulfill the opportunity—and all mankind will be the beneficiary of your courage.

FRANKLIN D. ROOSEVELT

Grateful debtors all of us, pilgrims from many far-off homes, we here commemorate the honored dead of Hyde Park, the home of Franklin Roosevelt. The hallowed places of our country are many. But this place is a shrine for the whole free world.

As with too few men, Franklin Roosevelt's home and home folk were a part of him and he of them. Here he was a solid countryman at heart, and as Churchill has said, a countryman used to natural catastrophe of flood and drought, lightning and storm, doesn't panic at human catastrophe.

All who lived here with him and all generations before him buried here contributed to what he was and what he did. We know he felt with Edmund Burke that society is a compact between the living, the dead, and those yet unborn, and a responsible statesman must at the same time respect and cherish all three.

A Time for Action

In all Franklin Roosevelt did to meet the turmoil of his times he was never afraid of catastrophe, natural or human. He knew there was nothing to fear but fear itself. And he never forgot that he was an instrument of the American dream.

Fifteen years after his death, we are getting some perspective, some insight into the over-all accomplishment of Franklin Roosevelt. It is too simple to say that he saved his nation and he saved his world. This we know. Already, this is clearly the verdict of history.

DEMOCRATIC FORMS AND REALITY

The more absorbing question is how he managed to meet the terrible problems of depression and war without sacrificing the traditional liberty and democratic forms of the simpler nineteenth-century civilization of America.

Revolution was in Roosevelt's day the order of the world. Only the English-speaking nations were able to meet their problems without sacrificing the form and the substance of parliamentary democracy. Italy substituted fascism, Russia international communism, Germany nazism, and Japan military dictatorship. All of these nations insisted upon, even glorified in, violence as a tool of state.

The glory of Roosevelt and the New Deal is, as

I have said, that their achievements, both in peace and in war, were through the democratic process.

THE MIDDLE CLASS

Our hindsight, as we stand in memory before his grave today, allows us to see that certainly one of the most enduring of his accomplishments has been the strengthening of the great American middle class. This is the group most devoted to democracy and to a parliamentary and judicial process.

Here in 1933, as elsewhere in the world, were a small handful of very rich and masses of poor and dispirited. The backbone of the nation, the home-owners, the merchants, and the small businessmen, professional men, were being ground into poverty.

Today almost all of America can be described as middle class in the best sense of the word. Our people are prosperous, devoted to home ownership and to private property, insistent on the preservation of their rights, strong and stable financially, demanding education for their children.

This is no happenstance, no latter-day miracle. It is the heritage of the New Deal. Roosevelt made money the servant and not the master of the people by his financial legislation. He promoted efficiency and economy in our lagging monopolies by such direct yardsticks as TVA. The productive machinery of our industries was stimulated first by the needs caused by the depression and second by the necessity of preparing ourselves for defense against the dictators of the world.

APPRENTICESHIP AND FULFILLMENT

How was he able as the only leader in the world to preserve the continuity between the past and the present and project it into the future?

Possibly just to live in government in New York State in the early period of his life was to anticipate the opportunities and the problems that were later to come to the whole nation and acquaint him with the new forces that were to transform the world. In his freedom from fear he not only refused to obstruct these new forces, he encouraged and expanded them.

Franklin D. Roosevelt was born almost in the year of the erection of the Statue of Liberty—the symbol of the immigrant—whose seventy-fifth anniversary was observed last year.

The most significant forces of his early years were the emigration from the East to the West and the immigration from old Europe to the New World. The fullest impact of these forces was felt first in New York. New York harbor was the important port of entry for the new immigrant. The Hudson

River and the Erie Canal were the most important routes west for hundreds of thousands of farm settlers into the great West.

The American state is the only one in history—with the possible exception of ancient Athens—which arranged for its own bloodless invasion, with the sole condition that the newcomers take on the American identity of all.

FUSION OF SPIRIT

In this seventy-fifth year of the Statue of Liberty, it is not too much to say that the Democratic party of Alfred E. Smith and Robert Wagner and Woodrow Wilson and the public schools were the means by which this fusion of spirit was accomplished. It is not too much to say that Franklin D. Roosevelt was both its master chemist—and its personal catalyst.

Neither he nor the Democratic party need look to the polls for vindication. The sons and daughters of these immigrants, gracing the highest places and councils of this nation, give full and magnificent answer every day of their highly useful and effective lives.

There were no underprivileged sections any more than classes, races, or creeds in his concept of the American dream. This he had received in trust from his fathers to improve for his own generation and to keep open for the future.

A NATIONAL PRESIDENT

He was a New Yorker and an Easterner. But one of the first tasks which he set himself was the raising up of the South, economic problem number one, still suffering from the destruction of capital in the War Between the States. He was an Easterner and a New Yorker but the second important task he set himself was to bring to the West the electric power, the rural electrification, and the water which it needed to grow. And the West and South will forever love him—and follow where he led.

Franklin D. Roosevelt knew that the development of individual talent was the key to national well-being, as the raindrop is to the brook, and the brook to the river. Our democracy as such is not only opposed to mediocrity; it may justly claim that its fair chance for individual development is the only system in the world which provides for the bloodless rise of a *functioning* aristocracy. By their works, not their words, shall ye know them. This is the measure of true aristocracy.

As the last generation saw the doors opened widely to all, for equal opportunity, the coming generations will apply the same standards to all, as befits a noble, competitive people.

LYNDON B. JOHNSON

VOICE OF HOPE

We need today to hear again the voice of Roosevelt through those whom he inspired and touched with fire. We need a voice that today gives hope and aspiration to the liberty-seeking peoples of Central Europe—to the Poles and Czechs and the divided German people behind the Iron Curtain. We need the same kind of hope that the Democratic party gave to the immigrant in Roosevelt's youth and that Roosevelt gave to a distraught and hopeless nation and world in his maturity. Our service at this shrine is a testimony to our faith as well as our hope that that voice will never die.

Here was the beginning—but here is not the end. Tens of thousands of people come to this shrine to renew their faith, as well as to pay their respect. All races, creeds, and nations are the better for his life —and of no man can more be said.

He was born an American, but he belongs to the world. Humbly, proudly, and reverently, we claim him as President Franklin D. Roosevelt of the United States of America. But his name, his great heart and spirit, and his magnificent life are a guardian in the skies—protecting his people whom he loved, always.

I am happy to bring to you from the people and the Government a message which is as absolutely determined and meaningful as it is simple to state.

That message is that the United States is resolved to do everything within its power—and I emphasize the word everything—to enhance the strength and unity of the North Atlantic community.

This message reflects the basic purpose of our foreign policy: to maintain an environment in which free societies can survive and flourish. By free societies we mean those in which the consent of the governed plays an important role.

It is essential to this environment that it be spacious. It is essential, too, that within it there should exist the will and power to protect it against enemies, and the opportunity for all to develop and to pursue happiness as they see it, within the limits of ability and willingness to work.

No single nation has enough influence and power

to maintain this spacious environment of freedom. The coalition of the peoples and nations of Western Europe and North America is indispensable to this end. Without their power—the resultant of population, resources, technology, and will—it cannot be preserved.

To the United States it is of prime importance to maintain and strengthen the coalition: both its cohesion and power within the Atlantic area and its capacity for constructive action outside that area.

If that cohesion and capacity are to be enhanced, vigorous measures will be required in the political, military, and economic fields.

In the political field it is to discover and act on the most basic of the various alliance interests that are at stake, and thus increase the alliance's capacity to influence events in the world at large constructively.

Progress toward an integrated European community will help to enhance that capacity and thus to strengthen the Atlantic community. A more cohesive and powerful Europe within a developing Atlantic community is needed to undertake the large tasks which lie ahead. The essentially national and loosely coordinated efforts of the past will no longer suffice.

Our end goal—"that remote and ideal object" of which Lord Acton spoke, "which captivates the imagination by its splendor and the reason by its simplicity"—should be a true Atlantic community in which common institutions will increasingly be developed to meet common problems.

The burgeoning demands of the less-developed countries no less than the growth of Soviet power dictate that a more tightly-knit community eventually be achieved. In progressing toward such a community, we can regain the sense of forward movement and imaginative thinking which has characterized the alliance in its most creative periods. In the long run, such progress may well prove to be indispensable if our ultimate goal of a free and orderly world community is to be achieved.

In the military field, too, the United States will do its utmost to sustain and enhance the strength of the alliance. I shall speak more briefly about this field, since these matters will soon be discussed in detail in the Council.

My country's approach to NATO's military tasks is governed by the principles which are reflected in the President's recent message to the Congress on our own military budget. Our objective is to insure that any potential aggressor will know that he would be confronted with a suitable, selective, swift, and effective military response.

To fulfill this objective, the United States is seeking to create a flexible and balanced military posture.

This is also the goal of NATO.

To achieve this goal, several steps will be called for.

For one thing, a vigorous and sustained effort to build up NATO's non-nuclear defenses will be required. This is a high priority task; it will call for increased effort from all of us. But the result will be worth the sacrifice, for NATO's defenses will be more effective and their deterrent power greater. As part of its contribution to this task, the United States is committed to full participation in the common defense and the maintenance of its military strength on the Continent for the foreseeable future. The President was absolutely clear on this point in his message to NATO soon after taking office.

An effective NATO nuclear capability is also needed to achieve our goal, and the United States stands ready to consult closely with all members of the alliance on the best ways and means of maintaining this capability in the future. The security of Europe and the security of the United States are inseparable.

In going forward with a practical and balanced program to strengthen NATO's arms, we will reduce any temptation to aggression and thus enhance the prospects for peace.

The fruits of peace are not achieved merely by

avoiding war. We must also seek to progress toward a richer life for all mankind.

If the Atlantic community is to help achieve that progress, we will need:

First, higher rates of growth in some Atlantic countries;

Second, more effective coordination between the economic policies of Europe and North America;

Third, increased aid to less-developed countries; and

Fourth, fair sharing within the alliance of the burden of that aid and of our military programs.

The OECD was created to help achieve just these purposes.

The United States intends to participate fully in its work to this end.

This is not the time or the place to go into the details. I wish only to lay out the general course of action to which we are dedicated, in seeking closer economic cooperation with our Atlantic partners.

We cannot fail in this course, if there is to be a high assurance of maintaining an environment in which free societies can flourish.

The effectiveness of the OECD in prosecuting this course will be an indispensable base both for the military programs which I have described and for fulfilling the purposes of the Atlantic community in less-developed areas.

The political impact of progress to this end may, however, be even more significant than its economic or military effect. For the chief Western nations will have been brought together into earnest conclave to launch measures of great and constructive moment. This would contribute to their confidence and cohesion and, over the long run, might well lay the basis for a new and ever closer relation between North America and Europe.

It would make more solid the hope that the world will be developed in peace—a secure and peaceful world in which international disputes can be straightened out in accordance with the Charter of the United Nations. I have just come from Geneva. We are earnestly striving to get a nuclear test ban treaty. We want and we pledge our best efforts to get a sound and effective treaty. If so, it may well be a prelude for constructive planning for disarmament.

If these hopes are frustrated, it must not be and will not be upon the conscience of the free world. We can and will have the satisfaction and knowledge that we labored diligently and we tried with dignity and honor, even if we pled in vain. A genuine political—as well as economic—community might appear increasingly feasible as our long-run goal.

Such a demonstration of the Atlantic nations' capacity for bold and creative effort could not fail also to impress mightily friendly nations in other areas, and possibly the communist leaders themselves. For its plain import would be to bring within reach the formation of what would be incomparably the most powerful economic grouping in the world. No calculation of the future relative strength of the free world could fail to be decisively affected by this prospect.

If we go forward with these general policies in the political, military, and economic fields, we can look forward to an Atlantic community which will increasingly fulfill the rich promise that its founders foresaw when they signed the treaty twelve years ago.

The task will not be easy. It will call for continuing sacrifices from all of us.

Sacrifices of resources.

Sacrifices of man-years spent in uniform.

Sacrifices of special interests.

Sacrifices of ancient concepts in the light of growing interdependence.

We cannot shrink from these sacrifices if we are to be worthy of the common civilization which we share.

The United States is prepared to play its full part. It accepts the responsibilities of leadership, both in projecting its own effort and in setting forth its view as to the tasks of the alliance as a whole.

The message that I bring you today is evidence of

its unreserved commitment to these tasks, which all of our countries will need to prosecute vigorously in the decade that lies ahead if their high purposes are to be achieved.

It is a privilege to be in your state and on your campus. But I thank you especially for the opportunity to participate in this commemoration of a great event in the history of man's humanity to man.

On January 1, 1863, one hundred years ago, the President of the United States issued an executive order which has been described as "an immortal blow for human freedom." Time has proved the immortality of that Emancipation Proclamation by President Lincoln. If that proclamation—like its author—now "belongs to the ages," the fulfillment of the spirit and true purpose of that proclamation is a responsibility which belongs to those of us who live today.

In his message to Congress regarding the Emancipation Proclamation, President Lincoln said eloquently: "In giving freedom to the slave, we assure freedom to the free—honorable alike in what we give, and in what we preserve."

His words were true. But, as Wendell Phillips

said of it "that proclamation frees the slave, but ignores the Negro." Those words also were true. Today, one hundred years later, it is the challenge, the duty, and the opportunity of our generation to direct our efforts toward overcoming the vestiges of what the Emancipation Proclamation of 1863 ignores.

To strike the chains of a slave is noble. To leave him the captive of the color of his skin is hypocrisy. While we in America have freed the slave of his chains, we have not freed his heirs of their color. Until justice is blind to color, until education is unaware of race, until opportunity ceases to squint its eyes at pigmentation of human complexions, emancipation will be a proclamation—but it will not be a fact. To the extent that the proclamation of emancipation is not fulfilled in fact, to that extent we shall have fallen short of assuring freedom to the free.

In these times, it is appropriate to recall at this observance that the Emancipation Proclamation itself was issued in the midst of a great struggle which divided our country one hundred years ago, as the world in which we live now is divided by an even greater struggle.

President Lincoln was counseled on many sides not to proclaim the freedom of the slaves until that struggle was won and the peace was made stable. To do so, he was told, would invite the danger of further secessions from the Union and impair the chances for success in the struggle to preserve the Union. But we today know the consequences. The Emancipation Proclamation was a turning point in the success of the Union's cause.

Directly and specifically as a result of President Lincoln's fidelity to the principles and ideals of our country's conception, world opinion and sympathy shifted to the support of the Union cause—and the ultimate success of that cause was assured.

Today, as then, we are engaged in a great struggle. We too hear counsel urging restraint and urging delay. We too are counseled that for the Government of the United States to concern itself with the equality of its citizens invites the risk of impairing the chance for success in our struggle to uphold the cause of freedom in the world.

The counsel of delay is not the counsel of courage. A government conceived and dedicated to the purpose that all men are born free and equal cannot pervert its mission by rephrasing the purpose to suggest that men shall be free today—but shall be equal a little later.

We are spending billions of dollars—tens of billions each year—to preserve freedom on this earth. Yet the annual economic cost of inequality among Americans—of discrimination by Americans against fellow Americans—costs more each year than the total of our budget for the exploration of outer space. To preserve freedom costs billions. To make progress toward equality costs mainly time, effort, and perseverance. If we can afford the billions, we can certainly afford the time, effort, and perseverance.

In speaking today as I do, I am personally aware that I speak as a grandson of Confederates to grandsons and great-grandsons of Union soldiers. I am aware, as an heir of Appomattox, that the barriers of bias and prejudice within our society are not all barriers of race and color—or of religion and creed. In our land, as in many lands, men know discrimination for the geography of their birth as well as the genetics of their birth.

But the point of our times is not that discrimination has existed—or that vestiges of it remain. But rather, the point is twofold: first, that we are making an effort in America to eradicate this cancer from our national life, and second, that we must proceed with dispatch in these efforts.

We may be white or Negro, northerner or southerner, Catholic, Protestant, or Jew—but the description is neither dual nor hyphenated, for the challenges before us require our unity as Americans. In the years of the twentieth century which remain before us, our country cannot meet what is expected and what is required of it unless and until we overcome those biases which exclude any from full participation in citizenship and productive effort on the basis of race, religion, or region of their birth.

We are in the midst of the greatest technical revolution in history. Of all the scientists who have ever lived, 90 per cent of them are alive today. More mathematics has been created since the beginning of the twentieth century than in all the rest of history combined. Ten years from now three-fourths of the people working in industry will be producing products not yet invented or discovered.

In this period, we in the United States face a problem which we have not as yet fully acknowledged—the pressing problem of our shortage of highly trained, fully educated manpower.

In 1955, the number of earned degrees in the physical sciences conferred in the United States at the bachelor's level numbered 10,516; at the master's level, 2,544; and at the doctor's level, 1,713. In 1961—despite the known need and increased demand from space, defense, and industrial research —the number of men and women receiving degrees in physical sciences had only climbed to 15,500 bachelors, 3,799 masters, and 1,991 doctors. This is progress, but not the progress we need to meet our needs. And to make the outlook worse, enrollment in the biological sciences, in engineering, and in other such fields has been declining rather than increasing during the last ten years.

The situation in medicine is grave. In 1955, 6,718 men and 338 women earned their M.D.'s, and in 1961 the graduates of medical schools numbered 6,648 men and again 338 women. That was a loss of seventy men entering one of our top-paying professions.

At the public school level, the United States is today losing one million students a year who quit high school before graduation. In the higher levels of education, 40 per cent of those who enter college drop out before completing the work for their degrees. By the 1970's, we must graduate 50 per cent more doctors than we are graduating now. We will need 7,500 Ph.D.'s in engineering, mathematics, and the physical sciences—compared to our total of such Ph.D.'s in 1960 of only 3,000. By 1970, we will need 80,000 graduate students in these subjects— and in 1960 we had only 34,000.

Time is already running out. Practically every student who could obtain a Ph.D. by 1970 is already enrolled in college now.

It is true that there are some who say that nothing more need be done, should be done, or can be done in this realm of support for education in America—but such views are not realistic. America's commitment to education as "the Guardian Genius of Democracy" is a commitment which has not yet been made and is not now being kept. We cannot

In 1954, Senate Democratic Leader Johnson
listens to President Eisenhower.

At the 1956 Democratic Convention LBJ
backs the leaders, old and new.

LBJ at Uvalde, Texas,
in 1958, with old
friends Truman, Garner,
and Rayburn.

The successful Democratic candidates in 1960.

On January 20, 1961, at the Inauguration of President Kennedy and Vice President Johnson.

A White House luncheon in 1961 brings together three winning Democrats.

At the Moffett Field research center, in 1961, Vice President Johnson visits with a member of the astronaut test group.

Vice President Johnson with an Indian village child during his visit to that country in June, 1961.

In Dakar, in April, 1961, Vice President Johnson visits with Senegal's poet-president, Leopold Senghor.

In July, 1962, the Vice President, who is also Chairman of the Advisory Council to the Peace Corps, discusses things with Peace Corps trainees in Puerto Rico.

Vice President Johnson has a private audience with Pope John XXIII in September, 1962.

On November 22, 1963, on an airplane heading for Washington, Lyndon B. Johnson is sworn in as President of the United States.

President Johnson addresses the joint session
of Congress on November 27, 1963.

long afford to continue on this course, for as Thomas Jefferson once wrote, "If you expect a nation to be ignorant and free, you will expect what never was and never will be."

To deal with this subject—and to recite these statistics—is to give attention to the principal sector of unfinished business for America since the Emancipation Proclamation of January 1, 1863. If America is to have the manpower resources which these later years of the twentieth century require, the diplomas of our high schools and the degrees of our colleges must not be "white" diplomas or "white" degrees.

America needs the resources of all its young minds without regard to color or heritage or religion or region.

In that Emancipation Proclamation, one hundred years ago, Abraham Lincoln said: "I hereby enjoin upon the people so declared to be free to abstain from all violence, unless in necessary self-defense; and I recommend to them that, in all cases when allowed, they labor faithfully for reasonable wages."

In our times today, our national self-interest requires that we go much beyond that language. It is not enough to recommend to any among the American family that they "labor faithfully for reasonable wages—in all cases when allowed." A determined national effort must continue to be made for the purpose—and with the objective of being certain:

That the talents of all are sought out and put to their highest use;

That opportunity and promotion come on the basis of ability;

That the highest rung on the ladder of our society be as accessible to all of talent and genius as are the lowest rungs.

It is our responsibility and our trust in this Year of Our Lord 1963 to strike the chains of bias and prejudice from minds and practices as Lincoln, a century ago, struck down slavery.

———————————————

Since the history of our country began, Americans have had a national characteristic of frequently over-estimating their adversaries and consistently under-estimating themselves.

In the twentieth century this characteristic has led us to be wrong time and time again in estimating our national capabilities for social progress. At the turn of the century—before the widespread use of the typewriter—the only work for women was in sweatshops. Child labor was accepted as a matter of course in the mines and factories—with children often beginning to work at the age of six or earlier.

While such conditions were certainly not enjoyed, there was a nearly unanimous feeling that such conditions could not and would never be changed. But in three decades of this century, the sweatshop was on its way out and exploitation of child labor had been largely ended.

Ten years later the early unionists were crusading against the sixty-hour week. Their goals seemed to be a highly impractical dream, because so many believed it would be contrary to the laws of God and nature for man to work on any schedule other than sun to sun. Yet, here again, in less than a decade the forty-hour week became universal.

What many believed could never be changed was changed in the twinkling of an eye as the history of the human race is measured. I believe it is important to the discussions of your conference here today to keep this perspective on the amazing capability of our free society to make—in a very short period— the achievements necessary to assure observance and fulfillment of the principles of human justice for which this nation was ordained and established.

It has been only in the last few decades that America has made a concerted effort to right the wrongs and correct the inequities of the status of its non-white citizens. We cannot as yet begin even to whisper the word success about those efforts. There is much to be done. And we should never become so complacent about how far we have come that we fail to realize how heartbreakingly far we have to go. But at the same time it is a disservice to our nation not to acknowledge fully and frankly that a very great deal has been done—and that we have attained real progress within the past several years.

In the fields of individual rights, political equality, education, and other sectors, the world of America's non-white citizens today scarcely resembles their world in 1940—or even in 1950. Traditionally the

Negro had been associated with and tied to the rural and agricultural sectors of our economy. But by 1960, 73 per cent—nearly three out of four—Negroes were living in urban areas.

In 1950, only 27 per cent of our non-white population had attained high school or college—compared to 54 per cent of the white population. In 1960, 40 per cent of the non-white population had acquired some high school or college education, compared to 62 per cent of the white population.

These are certainly not conclusive figures—and they are not figures with which we can be satisfied. But these figures do indicate how rapid our rate of gain has become.

I mentioned a moment ago that it is a disservice to our country to ignore or deny the progress that is being achieved. The greatest disservice, however, is to the group of young Americans with whom this conference is mainly concerned—our young Negro citizens.

Educational opportunities are open to their generation which have been open to no Negro generations before them. But the young Negroes of the 1960's are faced with a contradiction—is the time and money required for taking advantage of these educational opportunities worth it in terms of what they can expect after high school, or especially after college?

LYNDON B. JOHNSON

A very great deal of the visible evidence would lead many young people to conclude that the answer is no. Case after case can be cited of Negroes of other generations who after attaining advanced degrees in sciences or the humanities have spent their lives as headwaiters in restaurants or bill collectors in metropolitan slums. Seeing these examples, it is not hard to understand why most young Negroes must debate the question whether the promise of a college degree is a hollow promise for them.

The question facing the young Negro today is not just the question of how much opportunity there will be in America in the future—but how much opportunity will there be for him. No one can give a final answer to that question. But if we look at our country's past—and at our country's present efforts—faith is justified. The most tragic mistake that a young Negro can make today is to decide that there is no basis for faith in the opportunity which the future will offer to him.

As each of you knows, it is my privilege to serve as chairman of the President's Committee on Equal Employment Opportunity. This committee is concerned—as its name implies—with the objective of making equal employment opportunity a reality for all our citizens regardless of race, religion, or national origin. We are now working in and with all sectors of our economy—labor unions as well as business, government agencies as well as private employers.

I believe it can be said objectively that as a direct result of programs initiated and directed by the committee, more progress toward meaningful employment opportunity has been made in the last two years than in the last twenty years, or perhaps the last two hundred years of our history.

The committee supervises strict nondiscriminatory orders covering twenty million workers in private industry working on government contracts.

The committee supervises nondiscriminatory programs covering the employment and working conditions of two and a half million federal employees.

Most of the major industrial corporations which contract with the federal government have voluntarily adopted and are applying Plans for Progress, which go even beyond the terms of the executive order in eliminating discrimination in hiring, training, promotion, and dismissal.

In this sector, invaluable progress is being made toward initiating programs aimed at doing more than merely observing the letter of equal employment agreements. In nearly twenty of our major industries the largest corporations are embarking upon projects to open employment doors which have never been opened before to Negroes and other minority groups, provide training which will permit promotion and advance for the individual without discrimination, and taking other such progressive steps.

In 1962, one hundred twenty AFL-CIO unions and three hundred directly affiliated unions signed fair practices agreements with the committee to eliminate discrimination similar to those in industry.

Impressive progress has been made toward making the federal government itself a showcase of opportunity. In the middle brackets of the civil service, the increase during the past year in Negro employment has been three times greater than the increase for the segment as a whole. At the upper levels of civil service, the increase has been four times greater.

It is not my thesis at all that these attainments are a cause of satisfaction or self-congratulation. On the contrary, I believe that this work has only just begun. But it is important that the generation of Negro youth now in or approaching high school or college have faith in what this progress will mean and in how rapid that progress will become.

The basic fact facing today's young Negro is that his nation is confronted in these last decades of the twentieth century with the most serious shortage of highly skilled manpower we have ever known. The appetite of American industry and government for college graduates has never been as great—and yet we are graduating too few advanced-degree students in the sciences and related fields today to meet even yesterday's demands. If we are realistic about it, this means that before the 1970's have come and gone, the opportunity for trained Negro youth will be the greatest in history—and room will be open for them at the top of the ladder, not on the bottom rungs alone.

The personal decisions which our young people must make now about continuing their education— or about the kind of careers for which they will prepare themselves—are crucial decisions. While in many fields the promise may at the moment seem to be blighted, the greater probability is that the young people will be blighting their own lives if, when the 1970's come, they find that decisions made today will have blighted their own personal opportunity for participation in the new world that will be open to them then.

We are faced today not with merely a compassionate interest in motivating young Negroes to prepare themselves for advanced careers—we have a national interest in doing so. The manpower needs of the next quarter century must be met if America is to retain its leadership for freedom in the world. We cannot afford to waste our human resources. We will not have the kind of society we want to have if large segments of our population are under-prepared for the opportunities which will be opened and accorded to them.

When we talk of motivation, we are basically talking of faith. The task before all of us—before you, before the industrial leaders of the nation, and certainly before the public officials of our land—is to inspire the young members of non-white groups in our society to have faith in the capacity and the will of their country to move forward in the realms of social progress and justice.

We who are working in this field at the federal level are acutely aware of the immediate need for success in this responsibility. This is not a case of motivating generations to come. There is an urgent need to inspire and lead the young Americans who are already in high school and in college to continue their personal preparation for the greater promise which the future will surely bring for them.

The strength of our society is this historic and traditional capacity to correct its own faults and rectify its own injustices. We are presently at the center of a most historic time in our efforts to improve the lot of the non-white citizens among us. The progress that we have made in the last fifteen years—and the effort we are able to apply to this field now—make it imperative that young Negroes, in their own self-interest, not bet against the future of their country or themselves.

To the Cleveland Urban League
Cleveland, Ohio
January 26, 1963

———————————————

Before coming here today, my good friend Secretary
Celebrezze cautioned me that even in a progressive
city like Cleveland I would be likely to find those
citizens who have a strong preference for lower
taxes—and strong feelings against a national deficit.
As you are well aware, the Administration which
both your former Mayor and I serve is now offering
both of those attractions. However, my purpose today is to talk with you of the cause and cure of a
national deficit which far exceeds that anticipated in
the federal budget for fiscal 1964.

I refer to the dollars-and-cents cost which our
country pays every year as the exorbitant price for
discrimination.

The Council of Economic Advisers calculates that
elimination of discrimination in our economy and
our society would add $15 billion to our gross na-
tional product each year. That is one-and-one-half
times more than the interest on the national debt;
three times more than the budget for Secretary

Celebrezze's Department of Health, Education, and Welfare; five times greater than military and economic assistance to other nations; and equal to nearly one-third the cost of our national defense.

In other words, we've got too many trained men and women working in jobs that require none of their skills, and all because of skin coloration.

I have emphasized these figures for a reason. We are observing this year the hundredth anniversary of the signing of the Emancipation Proclamation. That proclamation stands as one of the noble documents of our history. When we talk about it, there is an understandable temptation to indulge in rhetoric and rolling phrases because it does inspire a justified eloquence.

At this time and place in our history, however, it is far more appropriate that we take a both-feet-on-the-ground view of the work which remains to be done in the spirit of that proclamation. Abraham Lincoln faced the issue of men in the bondage of chains. A century later, we who live today face the issue of men in bondage to the color of their skins. The Emancipation Proclamation freed the slaves— but it did not free America of the burdens or the costs of discrimination.

We are today confronted with the challenge of those costs—and of overcoming them. President Lincoln recognized that "a house divided against itself cannot stand." Our challenge is to recognize that a people discriminating against themselves can neither prosper to the fullest of their potential nor enjoy together the full fruits of domestic tranquillity and freedom.

As Vice President of the United States, it is my privilege to serve as chairman of two Presidential committees—the President's Committee on Equal Employment Opportunity and the National Aeronautics and Space Council.

These two positions serve constantly to impress upon me both the magnitude of the challenge America faces in regard to discrimination and the opportunity which this present period in our national affairs presents for solution of that challenge.

Our national space effort today is great—and it is growing. We face many problems of technology. But the greatest problem which hangs over this national effort is the question of where we get the quantity and quality of manpower America will need throughout the remaining years of this century.

When the twentieth century began, American industry had two hundred factory workers for each engineer. Today, the national average is about fifty to one. In some industries, it is ten to one.

The demands of the Space Age are accelerating the shift in this ratio at an incredible rate. This is illustrated by Project Mercury, which has sent three

Americans into orbit around the earth. Project Mercury is less than five years old. In that short period, however, it has already created tens of thousands of new jobs in our economy—and it is estimated that more than 400,000 workers have made contributions to that project.

While Project Mercury is still operating, Projects Gemini and Apollo are developing with the objective of landing a man on the moon. Hundreds of thousands of additional trained and skilled craftsmen in many fields will be needed to make these projects successful.

This will be the pattern throughout the future. But the question remains: where do we get the quantity and quality of manpower we need?

By 1970—only seven years away—we will be needing 7,500 Ph.D.'s in engineering, mathematics, and the physical sciences. In 1960, only 3,000 Ph.D.'s were awarded. By 1970 we shall need 30,000 graduate students in those same fields. Last year we had only 10,000 such graduate students enrolled.

Ninety per cent of all scientists who have ever lived in the history of the world are living today. In less than ten years, 75 per cent of the persons working in the industry of America will be producing products that have not yet been invented or discovered. We are racing against time in the effort to maintain the quality of manpower supply we shall need. For example, practically every student who could obtain a Ph.D. by 1970 has already entered college.

While these are our needs, we are faced with the fact that in our public education system about one million students are quitting high school each year without graduating. Many of these wouldn't go on to college but many of them could do better by staying in school and learning to run a lathe or a card-punch machine.

The fact is obvious that if we are to meet our needs, a large part of the answer must come and will come from eliminating the discrimination which deprives us of the full use of the talents of young non-white Americans.

Our strength as a nation—and our success as a world leader in the cause of freedom—depends upon the responsibility, the diligence, and the speed with which we attack the problems of unequal opportunity in the practices of our economy and our society.

I am pleased by the fact that so many of the nation's large employers—including many firms with plants in the Cleveland area—are voluntarily facing this problem and undertaking to do something about it. Most of the leading industrial corporations in the United States have adopted Plans for Progress, pledging to take affirmative steps above and beyond requirements in eliminating discrimination in hiring, training, advancement, and promotion. I would like especially to mention a distinguished Ohio businessman who has made a valuable contribution as a member of the Presidential Committee—Mr. Fred Lazarus, Jr., of Cincinnati, Chairman of the Board of Federated Department Stores.

American industry is taking an intelligent and responsible view of the problem and of its own responsibilities. The unions of America, likewise, are accepting their share of responsibility. I am glad to say that the agencies of the federal government are making very substantial progress.

This is good—this is encouraging. But the demands of the next decade are pressing down upon us today. We shall not be able to meet those demands unless we can succeed at motivating young non-white Americans to pursue the studies, continue the classroom work, and otherwise prepare for the opportunities which will be open to them tomorrow.

The average Negro in America has had three years less schooling than the average white American. The long-standing pattern of job discrimination has discouraged Negroes from seeking to enter the mainstream of American industry and commerce. Too often in the past, Negroes with college degrees have been denied the opportunity to fulfill their capabilities and have been faced with the choice of continuing to work in the Negro community or accepting menial work in white-owned businesses.

When the work of the Committee on Equal Employment Opportunity began, the major task was that of persuading employers to utilize the talents of the well-trained Negro. Today, it is our new task— for our committee and for your organization—to convince the Negro himself that skills and training and education are worth acquiring.

We can compliment ourselves on the progress which has been made by organizations such as the Urban League and the Greater Cleveland Youth Service Planning Commission and others, without at the same time becoming falsely content with such accomplishments. These next hundred years of our national experience demand of us that we resolve the problems left unresolved when the Emancipation Proclamation freed the slaves. It is important for us to remember that we are working against time and that our efforts today must move forward with new determination, new dispatch, and new diligence if we are to succeed in giving America the full strength of all its people.

Let us continue the fight for equal opportunity, not as members of any race, but as Americans devoted to the goal of "one nation under God, indivisible, with Liberty and Justice for all."

THE CENTURY OF
HUMAN RIGHTS

You do me a very great honor by this award tonight. For deeply personal reasons, it is a most gratifying honor—most gratefully received—and I thank you for it.

In responding to what has been so generously said, I realize that I cannot divorce my personal words from my public station nor can I disregard the public nature of this occasion. But insofar as it is possible, I would like to speak with you as I might do privately.

This century in which we live has been given many names. One predecessor in the office I hold described it eloquently as the Century of the Common Man. Others have applied different descriptions of both hope and despair. For myself, I feel it may be most accurately and aptly described as the Century of Human Rights.

It may seem paradoxical to refer to a century which has seen the rise of two of the greatest tyrannies in history—fascism and communism—as the Century of Human Rights. But in the light of historic human behavior, it becomes apparent that there is no paradox whatsoever—in fact, that the rise of these forces is evidence of the growing strength of the cause of equality.

The intense fury with which the totalitarians of both the right and the left deny the concept of human rights is the measure of their realization that their cause is doomed. People who are truly confident, people who truly believe they represent the wave of the future, do not resort to mass denial of age-old religious practices, mass denial of political rights, or mass extermination. These are the weapons of frustration—the last resort of men who know, however loudly they may deny the fact, that they have reached the end of one of the blind alleys of history.

It is difficult for our generation—which has known of Dachau and Warsaw, of the imprisonment of cardinals, and the fate of Passover in the Soviet Union—to realize the tremendous advance of the concept of equal rights in the mid-twentieth century.

A few short decades ago the thought that *all* men

and women—regardless of race, creed, color, or origin—were entitled to equality of treatment was a novel idea. There was a concept of tolerance, but to far too many people it was a tolerance for "lesser breeds without the law," who were to be treated with kindness and humanity but not with equal regard as fellow beings.

There are very few thinking men today who regard this kind of tolerance as a virtue, however much it may have contributed at one time to "peaceful" relations. The whole moral drive of the Western world is focused on the concept that we are all children of God—however we may worship our God—and entitled to judgment on our individual merits without regard to irrelevant considerations of ancestry.

This is the true "wave of the future"—the fulfillment of the dreams and hopes of moral men throughout the ages. However much we may fall short of our ideals, we are striving to attain them with an intensity heretofore unknown to history. They have become an accepted part of the fabric of our society. And however vehement may be the forces of bigotry, the fact remains that those forces are on the defensive. They are fighting a losing battle.

That is why I am confident that our century—the Century of Human Rights—will be remembered for the legacy it leaves to the future more than for its inheritance from the past.

SEASON OF CHANGE

I would like to speak for these few moments about certain of our special American responsibilities to the greater fulfillment of this Century of Human Rights.

It is abundantly clear that in the course of our nation's affairs, we have arrived at a season of change in our policies and our relationships with the world—especially the non-Communist world. A period of searching reassessment has begun. However, we lose—and others lose—a necessary and indispensable perspective, when we neglect the fact that this is also a time for reassessment by all nations of the free world community.

All of us together are emerging from a period which has seen history's greatest explosion of political rights. We are also emerging from the early phase of what has been called the explosion of economic aspirations. In a very brief period, new world standards of political equality and equality of economic expectations have been established and we cannot neglect the implications.

We of America welcome what has happened. We are proudly conscious that both the revolution of political independence and the revolution of economic expectations had their beginning on these shores. We are conscious of special responsibilities to these forces which have reshaped the destinies of so many men. Our national policies since World War II have sought to honor those special responsibilities.

As the authentic revolutionaries of the world, however, we of America must make it clear to those who have chosen freedom that the revolution of freedom is fundamentally and above all else a revolution of human rights. And we must make it clear not only by words, but by example and precept. Our own house must be in order.

HARD DECISIONS

When our system was created, many hard decisions were required. None was harder—none was more revolutionary—than the decision embodied in our Bill of Rights that the central government should be prohibited from serving as the instrument for perpetuation of the prejudices and bias and discrimination of any sect or segment of American society. This decision was—and has continued to be—fundamental to our American unity, fundamental to our American capacity for economic growth, fundamental to the eternal harmony of our society, and fundamental to our capacity for exercising leadership on behalf of freedom beyond our own shores.

We must not acquiesce passively to any concept that the world can enjoy a new freedom while remaining the accomplice and prisoner of old prejudices.

To say this is to point no finger of scorn—nor to cast first stones of criticism. We make for ourselves no claim of national perfection.

But if a better world is to be built—and I am an unreserved optimist about the potentials—there must be a universal recognition that mankind must marshal the full potential of human resources and make full use of those potentials without regard to hereditary bias, prejudice, and discrimination.

If we of America are to rise to our full height as men in this century, we must face courageously the world's problem of human discrimination. We must speak clearly. We must speak in concrete terms. We must help the world to understand that the curing of the problems of discrimination is the beginning—not the end—of genuine freedom.

STEREOTYPES

As long as there have been societies more complex than tribal simplicity, majorities and minorities have relied on stereotypes to mold their opinions of one another. Such stereotypes have been convenient —but they have also been cruel.

We can take some measure of satisfaction from the fact that there *is* progress and that these stereotypes disappear as human understanding spreads.

For example, the two highest elective offices in the strongest free nation on earth are held today by men who have overcome the dead hand of the stereotype—for reasons of religion or region of birth. And I believe that each passing day will diminish the force of the stereotype for all of us.

As recently as last week, when I attended the swearing in of an Ambassador of the United States, it was noted in some accounts that I am "from a Southern state." The Ambassador himself was from a Southern state, also. But the accident of my birth became newsworthy, as did his, because I was born in the South of white parents—and he was born of Negro parents.

If to stand by his side and to shake his hand and to wish him "Godspeed" makes news, then that is news I am proud to make.

HIGHER SIGHTS

I say this to emphasize that the effort made by your national leadership today against discrimination, against bias, against division, and against the tyranny of stereotypes is, above all, an effort directed by men who know personally the enemy—and know his toll.

But I say this also to suggest that perhaps we of America should consider raising our sights toward larger horizons. Certainly in this field there is much still to accomplish—but what remains undone does not detract from the magnitude of what has been done.

Much of our effort is directed today to the subtle forms of discrimination. This is a necessary and worthwhile effort—and we cannot be content until we have succeeded completely. But when we look to the world as a whole, the problem of discrimination is a massive problem—requiring massive effort on our part.

We cannot be content until we commit ourselves to massive support of the cause of human rights everywhere.

Our American vocabulary is filled with frequent expressions identifying illiteracy, illness, ignorance, and poverty as the oppressors of humankind. I believe we need to complete our vocabulary by acknowledging frankly that the greatest oppressor of all continues to be that of bias and prejudice.

We shall have failed our country and our cause if, from the position we are now privileged to enjoy in the world, we do not undertake the initiative in fulfilling the promise of this twentieth century as the Century of Human Rights.

If we are to be remembered as constructive builders of a better world of peace and justice and freedom, we shall be remembered not for the dollars we send abroad but for the force of the influence and leadership we exercise to improve the lot of all mankind. It is this work that challenges us— it is this undertaking that summons us—it is toward this higher goal that we must lift up our sights and set our course.

EQUALITY OF
OPPORTUNITY

I can respond to your generosity tonight in two ways—and two ways only. First, I can express my deep and heartfelt thanks, and second, I can pray that I shall always conduct myself in such a way as to justify and merit your confidence.

It is only through the second response that I can—in any manner—approach levels of adequacy. Of this I am deeply conscious. The purpose of this meeting tonight is not to touch off a round of mutual backscratching congratulations. It is, instead, to review what has been done by some people in the hope that we can inspire ourselves and others to do even more.

I am very proud—and I do not apologize for my

pride—that you have included me in the company of those who are being honored tonight. At the same time, however, I am aware that this dinner does not represent the last chapter in a book or even the last page of a chapter. When we are involved in the field of human rights, we cannot consider the volume closed until those rights are so secure that no one even thinks of challenging them.

ROLL OF ACHIEVEMENT

At this moment in the history of our country, it is possible to call a roll of successful achievements in the struggle for equality of opportunity and human understanding. That roll can and should be called frequently because it is essential in times of strife and turmoil to remind ourselves that progress *is* possible and our goals some day *will* be achieved —if we have sufficient dedication.

But we would be doing ourselves and our country a disservice if we assumed that those successes meant that full and complete justice has been achieved. Quite the contrary! Justice is not a partial thing which can be measured in terms of percentages. Any degree of injustice is complete injustice. And until we achieve complete justice, we can regard progress only as a series of steps toward the goal. Each step should hearten us, but should not lull us into self-satisfaction that the job has been done.

Some months ago, the President's Committee on Equal Employment Opportunity, which I have the honor to head, released some statistics on minority group employment. They were "good" statistics in that they demonstrated a substantial improvement in the hiring practices of some of the firms that come under one of the committee's programs. It was a report of solid, substantial progress.

A Negro editor wrote an editorial for his newspaper the following week. Commenting on the figures, he said something like this: "When somebody points out how far I have come, I am the ungrateful kind of SOB who points out how far he has got to go."

Some people considered the comment to be ungracious—and perhaps it was. But that point did not bother me. The thought that loomed largest in my mind was that the comment was *valid*—and that the editor was absolutely right!

A SOBERING THOUGHT

A massive federal effort, backed by all the prestige of the executive agencies of the government, had succeeded only in bringing the editor (speaking figuratively) part-way along the road to a goal where he had a *right,* as a human being, to be without any federal effort at all.

This is a sobering thought which I commend to those of my fellow Americans who sometimes feel that efforts at progress should be abandoned because the presumed beneficiaries of these efforts do not express deep gratitude.

The truth of the matter is that there is nothing to be grateful for—except, perhaps, the discovery that decades of inequality have not succeeded in quenching the flame of conscience in the breast of our fellow man.

We are not trying to "do something" for a group of people that will give them an extra edge in life. All we are trying to do is to eliminate deprivation so this group will have an opportunity to compete with their fellow Americans on terms of equality. And should we succeed, I am confident that they will take care of themselves—as they want to anyway.

But the sands of time are running out. The hours are short and we have no moral justification in asking for an extension or a continuance.

As a prudent (at least, I hope I am prudent) man, I know that frequently in life I have had to settle for progress short of perfection. I have done so because—despite cynics—I believe that half a loaf *is* better than none. But my acceptance has always been conditioned upon the premise that the half-loaf is a step toward the full loaf—and that if I go on working, the day of the full loaf will come.

It seems to me that in the field of human rights, we are well past the stage where half a loaf will do. No one in this audience is so unrealistic as to expect to awake tomorrow morning in a perfect world. But, nevertheless, progress must come faster and I believe it will come faster as sensible men and women realize that they cannot afford—morally or economically—to abandon the field to the forces of unreason.

PROGRESS MUST BE FASTER

Progress must come faster because otherwise there are millions of individuals—human beings entitled to their rights—who will never receive justice, even though someday justice may come to their group.

Progress must come faster because otherwise the tragic headlines which speak of the breakdown of law and order will increase rather than diminish. (And I hope we relearn the lesson that issues which are not settled by justice and fair play will sooner or later be settled by force and violence.)

Progress must come faster because otherwise we

will not achieve the unity which we must have if freedom—freedom for all of us—is to survive.

And, finally, progress must come faster simply because it is right—and has been too long delayed.

UNDERSTANDING EAR

I think that one of the greatest barriers to progress is the fact that we don't talk to each other enough—or rather that we don't listen to each other enough with an understanding ear. We leap to conclusions too rapidly; we seize upon half-truths without looking at the full picture; we accept slogans without looking behind those slogans to the essential reality.

For example, it is said repeatedly that no law can enforce human understanding or implant reasonable attitudes among human beings. With this statement, I agree. It is valid. It is also beside the point and totally irrelevant to the issues that divide our country today.

The law cannot bring reasonable men and women together to work out their differences. But it can restrain unreasonable men and women from imposing their will on a community—and then the reasonable people *can*, and *will*, get together and work out their problems themselves.

The law cannot inject goodness and brotherhood

into those who are determined to reject both qualities. But it *can* prevent the extremists from trampling over the rights of others.

The law cannot "make men equal" and does not pretend to do so. But it *can* open the doors of equal opportunity which have been slammed shut by those who fear that when men and women *can* compete on an equal basis and *are* equal before the law, they will turn out to be rather equal after all.

And I want to make one point clear—very clear. This Administration is determined to enforce the law.

TO ENFORCE THE LAW

We are fully aware of the fact that the ultimate solutions must spring from the people themselves. But that is not—and will not be—an excuse for sitting idly by while minorities obstruct the efforts of just and reasonable men and women to find solutions.

I am not here tonight to make a speech. I am here to share this evening with you—to say thanks for your courtesy and to extend in return my best wishes.

I only wish to leave you with one thought. These are difficult, emotion-ridden times. We face strife

—and it is idle to pretend that it will go away. It is going to be difficult to maintain our perspective— at times virtually impossible.

Yet this we must do.

We must remember that we are all Americans— Americans with a difficult problem. We must work it out together. We must not be satisfied just with "progress," but neither can we afford to despair and reject progress.

I have faith that the day will come when it is not necessary nor remarkable to give or receive human rights awards—not necessary nor remarkable simply because justice will be color-blind and all men and women will be judged on their merits and not on irrelevant considerations of ancestry.

Thank you.

Memorial Day Address
Gettysburg, Pennsylvania
May 30, 1963

On this hallowed ground, heroic deeds were performed and eloquent words were spoken a century ago.

We, the living, have not forgotten—and the world will never forget—the deeds or the words of Gettysburg. We honor them now as we join on this Memorial Day of 1963 in a prayer for permanent peace of the world and fulfillment of our hopes for universal freedom and justice.

We are called to honor our own words of reverent prayer with resolution in the deeds we must perform to preserve peace and the hope of freedom.

We keep a vigil of peace around the world.

Until the world knows no aggressors, until the arms of tyranny have been laid down, until freedom has risen up in every land, we shall maintain our vigil to make sure our sons who died on foreign fields shall not have died in vain.

As we maintain the vigil of peace, we must remember that justice is a vigil, too—a vigil we must keep in our own streets and schools and among the lives of all our people—so that those who died here on their native soil shall not have died in vain.

One hundred years ago the slave was freed. One hundred years later the Negro remains in bondage to the color of his skin. The Negro today asks, "Justice." We do not answer him—we do not answer those who lie beneath this soil—when we reply to the Negro by asking, "Patience."

It is empty to plead that the solution to the dilemmas of the present rests on the hands of the clock. The solution is in our hands. Unless we are willing to yield up our destiny of greatness among the civilizations of history, Americans—white and Negro together—must be about the business of resolving the challenge which confronts us now.

Our nation found its soul in honor on these fields of Gettysburg one hundred years ago. We must not lose that soul in dishonor now on the fields of hate.

To ask for patience from the Negro is to ask him to give more of what he has already given enough. But to fail to ask of him—and of all Americans— perseverance within the processes of a free and responsible society would be to fail to ask what the national interest requires of all its citizens.

The law cannot save those who deny it, but neither can the law serve any who do not use it. The history of injustice and inequality is a history of disuse of the law. Law has not failed—and is not failing. We as a nation have failed ourselves by not trusting the law and by not using the law to gain sooner the ends of justice which law alone serves.

If the white overestimates what he has done for the Negro without the law, the Negro may underestimate what he is doing and can do for himself with the law.

If it is empty to ask Negro or white for patience, it is not empty—it is merely honest—to ask perseverance. Men may build barricades—and others may hurl themselves against those barricades—but what would happen at the barricades would yield no answers. The answers will only be wrought by our perseverance together. It is deceit to promise more, as it would be cowardice to demand less.

In this hour, it is not our respective races which are at stake—it is our nation. Let those who care for their country come forward, North and South, white and Negro, to lead the way through this moment of challenge and decision.

The Negro says, "Now." Others say, "Never." The voice of responsible Americans—the voice of those who died here and the great man who spoke here—their voices say, "Together." There is no other way.

Until justice is blind to color, until education is unaware of race, until opportunity is unconcerned with the color of men's skins, emancipation will be a proclamation but not a fact. To the extent that the proclamation of emancipation is not fulfilled in fact, to that extent we shall have fallen short of assuring freedom to the free.

At the Tufts University
Commencement Exercises
Medford, Massachusetts
June 9, 1963

THE CENTURY OF
THE EDUCATED MAN

When we stood about as far before the mid-point
of the century as we now stand beyond that point,
the twentieth century was popularized as the Century of the Common Man.

Today the year 1999 will soon be nearer to us
than the year 1929. We can see our times in a new
perspective. At this vantage point, it seems no longer
adequate to describe this as the Century of the
Common Man.

It is true that during these sixty-three years, the
common man on every continent has covered himself with glory. He has formed more nations, established more self-government, cast more ballots, built
more schools, studied more books, cured more disease, ministered to more needy than ever before.
The Century of the Common Man has also, as

Winston Churchill expressed it, been distinguished by "more common men killing each other with greater facilities than in any other five centuries put together."

The common man has been the focus of great economic and political revolutions. His status as an individual has changed. His institutions have changed. But today a new revolution is running—deeper, broader, more profound, and more permanent. It is a revolution of education, a revolution changing the capabilities of the common man—changing what he is, what he can be, and what his children after him will be. In this perspective, I believe we have come to a time when the century in which we live should henceforth be known as the Century of the Educated Man.

On a global basis, no statistics are adequate to suggest the magnitude of today's revolution of education. In our nation's programs overseas, thirty million people annually use the libraries we provide. We distribute eight million books abroad each year. The Soviet distributes twenty times more. But together these programs do not begin to meet the world demand.

Mere facts and figures cannot convey the human passion committed to the quest for learning. In our English-language teaching programs, small children in Latin America have sold the shoes off their feet to pay their way to classes—which they attend barefoot. In Africa, a tribal chief was turned away from enrolling in a class because there were no more chairs. The next day, he and a contingent of his fellow chiefs were waiting outside the door—each carrying his own chair.

This is not a revolution limited to other continents. Here in our own land, we have more than fifty million students attending more than 135,000 public and private schools at all levels. There are more students today in the United States than there were city residents only forty years ago.

Our American commitment to education is old and long-standing. But the real impact has just begun to come within very recent years.

We have entered an age in which education is not just a luxury permitting some men an advantage over others. It has become a necessity without which a person is defenseless in this complex, industrialized society.

Levels of education which were once regarded with awe have now become commonplace. And jobs which once could be filled by strength and native intelligence now call for a college degree. We have truly entered the Century of the Educated Man.

It is a mistake, however, to confuse skill with education. A man who has been taught only to hold a job has not been educated—he has been trained.

And the man who has merely been trained is not fully qualified to take his place in a free society as a fully participating citizen.

Education, of course, is not something that is acquired just in college. All of life is an education process and when I think of death, I think of it as the moment when the brain ceases to inquire and to expand.

There was a time when some Americans regarded an education just as a passport to a position of luxury in our society. We have come a long way from those days. We have learned that no man can avoid the obligations of citizenship—indeed, that these obligations are forced upon him.

This thought is particularly compelling at this time in our history when our country is torn by internal tensions.

People who have been denied basic rights for centuries have reached the explosion point where they are demanding those rights—now. And it is not possible to find logical, moral reasons to say them nay.

In the course of their struggle, government can—and, I assure you, will—protect them, as it protects all citizens, in the exercise of those rights which are guaranteed to them by the Constitution and the laws of the land. But the response to their real—and just —aims must come from the community as a whole.

Government will play its proper role. But our

citizens, though they may look to government for leadership, cannot abdicate their moral obligation to make a total commitment—and carry out that commitment—to the cause of equal opportunity and equal treatment for all Americans, regardless of irrelevant considerations of ancestry.

The days that lie ahead of us will be not only troubled, but confusing. The question of equal rights and equal treatment is not a simple one because it is complicated by traditions and patterns of thought that are deeply ingrained. The cause of a strong and united America will not be served by promoting misunderstanding and by refusing to understand the legitimate demands of those who are seeking simple justice.

We have too much of a tendency to equate the struggle for equal rights with social prestige and status. The issue is clouded by stating it in terms of who can live in what fashionable section and who can go into what desirable restaurant or who can go into what prestige school.

Frankly, it is difficult for me to see why anyone should deny to another person the right to any prestige to which he is entitled. But even beyond that, we must face up to the fact that individual economic survival in our modern industrial nation urgently demands equal access to the facilities of our society.

If we deny a man access to the education to which

he is entitled by capacity, we also deny him access to his rightful place in our economy. And, I might add, we also deny ourselves his productive skills.

If we deny a man access to adequate housing in an area of his choice, we restrict also his right to live with his family near the place where he can work.

If we restrict the right of a man to enjoy the ordinary comforts of life, we also restrict his right to move from one place to another in search of the best job for which he is qualified. In addition, we restrict the right of the employer to search out the best qualified worker.

Let us be very clear on this matter. If we condemn people to inequality in our society, we also condemn them to inequality in our economy. And we do our conscience a disservice if we dismiss their demands for social justice as a mere desire for social status.

I doubt very much whether those who have been the victims of discrimination have a burning desire to "mingle" with those who have oppressed them. I would think they have accumulated too many resentments. They probably wish that we would just go away and leave them alone.

But we live in a time when our country cannot be divided—not between slave and free or black and white. If we cannot permit each man and woman to find the rightful place in a free society to which they are entitled by merit, we cannot preserve a free society itself.

This is the challenge which faces this generation in the Century of the Educated Man.

One hundred years ago, we settled the question of whether men and women could be property. The answer was "No"—an answer that came through blood and agony.

But we did not—despite noble words and noble motives—settle the question of whether men and women would be equal in opportunity. We postponed that issue—simply because it did not force itself upon us in an agrarian society.

We are now learning that no moral issue can be postponed indefinitely. We did not settle the question on the basis of justice and equity when we had time to do so. Now we find we must settle it with turmoil and agony.

The settlement will be one that will try the souls and hearts of all men of all races and religions— north, south, east and west. This is not a sectional problem, because our society is unequal in every section. No part of our country is so without sin that it can cast the first stone.

And somehow we must maintain our compassion —not only for the victims of discrimination, but for those who are bewildered and frightened by the changes that are coming at such a fast pace. If we lose our compassion, we will merely substitute one injustice for another—and our agony will be in vain.

This is not a time for retribution but for justice.

The task before us is truly one for the educated mind because the educated mind sees things not only clearly but compassionately. Otherwise, that mind is merely trained. We are dealing with humanity, and if we do not treat people as human beings, the educated mind is a sham and a fraud.

This ceremony is quite properly called "Commencement." In a sense it is the commencement of your education and the commencement of your real problems.

You are stepping out into a world of danger. But where there is danger, there is also opportunity—and the greater the danger, the greater the opportunity.

I do not presume to give you advice because my generation cannot tell your generation that we faced up to all problems, solved all issues, and conquered all injustice.

But you are graduating in a time for greatness. I envy you the opportunity and I wish you well.

PROTECTION OF LIBERTY

On this honored day, here before this historic hall, we come together to celebrate the birth of our country. Yet it is the special privilege of our generation to know that this is not the cradle of liberty for Americans alone—it is, in a far larger sense, the cradle of liberty and independence for all mankind.

What was wrought here in the eighteenth century has changed the world in this twentieth century. To the farthest corner of the globe, men inspired by the Declaration of Independence have themselves declared their own independence. Fifty new nations have been created since World War II. None has chosen to adopt the communist system, but many have adopted the ideas—and even the very language—of the great documents of our American heritage.

Of this we can be justly proud. But the patriot is

not content with pride alone—he is concerned first and always with performance. This is the challenge our system and our society lay before all Americans today.

We are challenged to measure ourselves—to measure our own performance today—by that eternal standard set forth on this fourth day of July in 1776:

> We hold these truths to be self-evident, that all men are created equal, that they are endowed by their Creator with certain unalienable Rights, that among these are Life, Liberty, and the pursuit of Happiness.

On those words of 1776—and on the belief those words express—history's strongest nation and most successful society has been built. By the meaning we give to those words in this year of 1963, the fate and future of our nation—and the success of the cause we are privileged to lead—may well be determined.

This is a challenge. It is not an indictment. Our system has not failed. It is not in danger of failing. Our national soul is not lost. It is not in danger of being lost. The standards of law and order are not coming down—on the contrary, we can believe that they are now rising higher. For our whole history has been a history of enlarging the protections of individual liberty, even as we are called and challenged to do once more today.

Hardly had the Constitution been written than the people demanded of their leaders the protections of their liberties embodied in the Bill of Rights. The sons and grandsons of the Founding Fathers were challenged to extend those protections to the slave. Their sons and grandsons were, in turn, petitioned in the streets and public places to extend equality to women as well as men. We, as their heirs, have been challenged no less forcefully to mobilize our arms, our resources, and our young men to protect the liberties of free men throughout the world.

It has been the destiny of each generation of Americans to make liberty more secure for all by making liberty more certain for each of us. This is clearly the great destiny—and great privilege—which we of this generation face in our own land now.

The words on which our nation stands—the words on which it has stood 187 years—are clear and unmistakable. We would demean ourselves, we would demean our patriotism, we would demean our dignity as free men, to interrupt the course of our national progress to enter upon a prolonged debate about either the meaning of those words—or the

145

obligation they impose upon us to honor and fulfill their meaning.

The words of the Declaration of Independence—the words of the Constitution of the United States—do not need to be further interpreted.

They need to be implemented—for all Americans.

But implementation is not the work of government alone.

Governments can never be more just than the hearts of those from whom they derive their just powers. If we are to enjoy a just and tranquil society, we must reach decisions in our private hearts even as we strive to reach decisions in our public policies. This is our real challenge today.

These times—the issues of this moment in our history—call out for men and women who love their country to step forward with responsible leadership to implement in our national life the ideals of our national literature.

In every state, in every community, in every American home, we have the capability to answer the needs of this moment. It is the responsibility of each individual to put those capabilities to work to secure the answers required for the success of our system and society.

If we as a nation are to stand up to our full height

in the world, we must be concerned with nobler things than denying one another the simple right to sit down in public places.

If we as a nation are to stay in front of the world, we must occupy ourselves with more important concerns than asking one another to step to the rear of public vehicles.

If we are to commit our arms, our resources, and the lives of our young men to support the right of free men to come and go without molestation or harassment to a free city such as Berlin, we can make no less a commitment to assure the right of all our fellow countrymen to come and go without embarrassment or harassment along the highways of America itself.

We of this generation have proved ourselves worthy heirs of those who assembled here on July 4, 1776. We, no less than they, have pledged "our Lives, our Fortunes and our Sacred Honor" to preserve for free men throughout the globe Life, Liberty, and the pursuit of Happiness. What we have done so courageously for others, let us now do proudly for ourselves.

This is the spirit of this Day of Independence— the spirit of America itself. For as Thomas Jefferson wrote in the last letter before he died on the fiftieth anniversary of this great day:

LYNDON B. JOHNSON

All eyes are opened, or opening, to the rights of man. . . . For ourselves, let the annual return of this day forever refresh our recollection of these rights and an undiminished devotion to them.

To a Joint Session
of the Congress
November 27, 1963

———————————

All I have I would have given gladly not to be standing here today.

The greatest leader of our time has been struck down by the foulest deed of our time. Today John Fitzgerald Kennedy lives on in the immortal words and works that he left behind. He lives on in the mind and memories of mankind. He lives on in the hearts of his countrymen.

No words are sad enough to express our sense of loss. No words are strong enough to express our determination to continue the forward thrust of America that he began.

The dream of conquering the vastness of space—the dream of partnership across the Atlantic—and across the Pacific as well—the dream of a Peace Corps in less-developed nations—the dream of education for all of our children—the dream of jobs for all who seek them and need them—the dream of care for our elderly—the dream of an all-out attack on mental illness—and above all, the dream of equal rights for all Americans, whatever their race or color—these and other American dreams have been vitalized by his drive and by his dedication.

And now the ideas and ideals which he so nobly represented must and will be translated into effective action.

Under John Kennedy's leadership, this nation has demonstrated that it has the courage to seek peace, and it has the fortitude to risk war. We have proved that we are a good and reliable friend to those who seek peace and freedom. We have shown that we can also be a formidable foe to those who reject the path of peace and those who seek to impose upon us or our allies the yoke of tyranny.

This nation will keep its commitments from South Vietnam to West Berlin. We will be unceasing in the search for peace; resourceful in our pursuit of areas of agreement, even with those with whom we differ; and generous and loyal to those who join with us in common cause.

In this age, when there can be no losers in peace and no victors in war, we must recognize the obligation to match national strength with national restraint. We must be prepared at one and the same time for both the confrontation of power and the limitation of power. We must be ready to defend the national interest and to negotiate the common interest. This is the path that we shall continue to pursue. Those who test our courage will find it strong, and those who seek our friendship will find it honorable. We will demonstrate anew that the strong can be just in the use of strength; and the just can be strong in the defense of justice.

And let all know we will extend no special privilege and impose no persecution. We will carry on the fight against poverty and misery, disease and ignorance, in other lands and in our own.

We will serve all of the nation, not one section or one sector or one group, but all Americans. These are the United States—a united people with a united purpose.

Our American unity does not depend upon unanimity. We have differences; but now, as in the past, we can derive from those differences strength, not weakness; wisdom, not despair. Both as a people and a government, we can unite upon a program, a program which is wise, just, enlightened, and constructive.

For thirty-two years Capitol Hill has been my home. I have shared many moments of pride with you, pride in the ability of the Congress of the United States to act, to meet any crisis, to distill from our differences strong programs of national action.

LYNDON B. JOHNSON

An assassin's bullet has thrust upon me the awesome burden of the Presidency. I am here today to say that I need your help; I cannot bear this burden alone. I need the help of all Americans, and all America. This nation has experienced a profound shock, and in this critical moment, it is our duty, yours and mine, as the government of the United States, to do away with uncertainty and doubt and delay, and to show that we are capable of decisive action; that from the brutal loss of our leader we will derive not weakness, but strength; that we can and will act and act now.

From this chamber of representative government, let all the world know and none misunderstand that I rededicate this government to the unswerving support of the United Nations, to the honorable and determined execution of our commitments to our allies, to the maintenance of military strength second to none, to the defense of the strength and the stability of the dollar, to the expansion of our foreign trade, to the reinforcement of our programs of mutual assistance and cooperation in Asia and Africa, and to our Alliance for Progress in this hemisphere.

On the twentieth day of January in 1961, John F. Kennedy told his countrymen that our national work would not be finished "in the first thousand days, nor in the life of this Administration, nor even perhaps in our lifetime on this planet. But," he said, "let us begin."

Today, in this moment of new resolve, I would say to all my fellow Americans, let us continue.

This is our challenge—not to hesitate, not to pause, not to turn about and linger over this evil moment, but to continue on our course so that we may fulfill the destiny that history has set for us. Our most immediate tasks are here on this Hill.

First, no memorial oration or eulogy could more eloquently honor President Kennedy's memory than the earliest possible passage of the civil rights bill for which he fought so long. We have talked long enough in this country about equal rights. We have talked for one hundred years or more. It is time now to write the next chapter, and to write it in the books of law.

I urge you again, as I did in 1957 and again in 1960, to enact a civil rights law so that we can move forward to eliminate from this nation every trace of discrimination and oppression that is based upon race or color. There could be no greater source of strength to this nation both at home and abroad.

And second, no act of ours could more fittingly continue the work of President Kennedy than the early passage of the tax bill for which he fought all this long year. This is a bill designed to increase our national income and federal revenues, and to provide insurance against recession. That bill, if passed without delay, means more security for those now working, more jobs for those now without them, and more incentive for our economy.

In short, this is no time for delay. It is a time for action—strong, forward-looking action on the pending education bills to help bring the light of learning to every home and hamlet in America; strong, forward-looking action on youth employment opportunities; strong, forward-looking action on the pending foreign aid bill, making clear that we are not forfeiting our responsibilities to this hemisphere or to the world, nor erasing executive flexibility in the conduct of our foreign affairs; and strong, prompt, and forward-looking action on the remaining appropriations bills.

In this new spirit of action, the Congress can expect the full cooperation and support of the executive branch. And in particular, I pledge that the expenditures of your government will be administered with the utmost thrift and frugality. I will insist that the government get a dollar's value for a dollar spent. The government will set an example of prudence and economy. This does not mean that we will not meet our unfilled needs or that we will not honor our commitments. We will do both.

As one who has long served in both houses of the Congress, I firmly believe in the independence and the integrity of the legislative branch. And I promise you that I shall always respect this. It is deep in the marrow of my bones. With equal firmness, I believe in the capacity and I believe in the ability of the Congress, despite the divisions of opinions which characterize our nation, to act—to act wisely, to act vigorously, to act speedily when the need arises. The need is here. The need is now. I ask your help.

We meet in grief, but let us also meet in renewed dedication and renewed vigor. Let us meet in action, in tolerance, and in mutual understanding. John Kennedy's death commands what his life conveyed—that America must move forward. The time has come for Americans of all races and creeds and political beliefs to understand and to respect one another. So let us put an end to the teaching and the preaching of hate and evil and violence. Let us turn away from the fanatics of the far left and the far right, from the apostles of bitterness and bigotry, from those defiant of law and those who pour venom into our nation's bloodstream.

I profoundly hope that the tragedy and the torment of these terrible days will bind us together in new fellowship, making us one people in our hour of sorrow. So let us here highly resolve that John Fitzgerald Kennedy did not live—or die—in vain. And on this Thanksgiving eve, as we gather together

LYNDON B. JOHNSON

to ask the Lord's blessing and give Him our thanks,
let us unite in those familiar and cherished words:

America, America,
God shed His grace on thee,
And crown thy good
With brotherhood
From sea to shining sea.

My fellow Americans: On yesterday, I went before the Congress to speak for the first time as President of the United States.

Tonight, on this Thanksgiving, I come before you to ask your help, to ask your strength, to ask your prayers that God may guard this Republic and guide my every labor.

All of us have lived through seven days that none of us will ever forget. We are not given the divine wisdom to answer why this has been, but we are given the human duty of determining what is to be, what is to be for America, for the world, for the cause we lead, for all the hopes that live in our hearts.

A great leader is dead; a great nation must move on. Yesterday is not ours to recover, but tomorrow is ours to win or to lose. I am resolved that we shall win the tomorrows before us. So I ask you to join me in that resolve, determined that from this midnight of tragedy, we shall move toward a new American greatness.

More than any generation before us, we have cause to be thankful on this Thanksgiving Day. Our harvests are bountiful, our factories flourish, our homes are safe, our defenses are secure. We live in peace. The good will of the world pours out for us, but more than these blessings, we know tonight that our system is strong—strong and secure. A deed that was meant to tear us apart has bound us together. Our system has passed. You have passed a great test. You have shown what John F. Kennedy called upon us to show in his proclamation of this Thanksgiving: that decency of purpose, that stead-fastness of resolve, and that strength of will which we inherit from our forefathers. What better conveys what is best for America than this?

On Saturday, when these great burdens had been mine only hours, the first two citizens to call upon me and to offer their whole support were Dwight D. Eisenhower and Harry S. Truman.

Since last Friday, Americans have turned to the good, to the decent values of our life. These have served us. Yes, these have saved us. The service of our public institutions and our public men is the salvation of us all from the Supreme Court to the states. And how much better would it be, how much more sane it would be, how much more decent and

American it would be, if all Americans could spend their fortunes and could give their time and spend their energies helping our system and its servants to solve your problems instead of pouring out the venom and the hate that stalemate us in progress.

I have served in Washington thirty-two years—thirty-two years yesterday. I have seen five Presidents fill this awesome office. I have known them well and I have counted them all as friends—President Herbert Hoover, President Franklin Roosevelt, President Harry Truman, President Dwight Eisenhower, and President John Kennedy.

In each Administration, the greatest burden that the President had to bear was the burden of his own countrymen's unthinking and unreasoning hate and division.

So, in these days, the fate of this office is the fate of us all. I would ask all Americans on this day of prayer and reverence to think on these things. Let all who speak and all who teach and all who preach and all who publish and all who broadcast and all who read or listen—let them reflect upon their responsibilities to bind our wounds, to heal our sores, to make our society well and whole for the tasks ahead of us. It is this work that I most want us to do: to banish rancor from our words and malice from our hearts; to close down the poison spring of hatred and intolerance and fanaticism; to protect our unity north and south, east and west; to hasten the day when bias of race, religion and region is no more; and to make the day when our great energies and decencies and spirit will be free of the burdens that we have borne too long.

Our view is outward, our thrust is forward, but we remember in our hearts this brave young man who lies in honored eternal rest across the Potomac. We remember him; we remember his wonderful and courageous widow whom we all love. We remember Caroline and John and all the great family who gave the nation this son and brother.

And to honor his memory and the future of the works he started, I have today determined that Station No. 1 of the Atlantic Missile Range and the NASA Launch Operation Center in Florida shall hereafter be known as the John F. Kennedy Space Center.

I have also acted today with the understanding and the support of my friend the Governor of Florida, Farris Bryant, to change the name of Cape Canaveral. It shall be known hereafter as Cape Kennedy.

On this Thanksgiving Day, as we gather in the warmth of our families, in the mutual love and respect that we have for one another, and as we bow our heads in submission to divine providence, let us also thank God for the years that He gave us inspiration through His servant, John F Kennedy.

Let us today renew our dedication to the ideals that are American. Let us pray for His divine wisdom in banishing from our land any injustice or intolerance or oppression to any of our fellow Americans, whatever their opinion, whatever the color of their skins—for God made all of us, not some of us, in His image. All of us, not just some of us, are His children.

And, finally, to you as your President, I ask that you remember your country and remember me each day in your prayers, and I pledge to you the best within me to work for a new American greatness, a new day when peace is more secure, when justice is more universal, when freedom is more strong in every home of all mankind.

———————————

We meet in a time of mourning, but in a moment of rededication. My nation has lost a great leader. This organization has lost a great friend. World peace has lost a great champion.

But John Kennedy was the author of new hope for mankind, hope which was shared by a whole new generation of leaders in every continent, and we must not let grief turn us away from that hope. He never quarreled with the past. He always looked at the future. And our task now is to work for the kind of future in which he so strongly believed.

I have come here today to make it unmistakably clear that the assassin's bullet which took his life did not alter his nation's purpose. We are more than ever opposed to the doctrines of hate and violence, in our own land and around the world. We are more than ever committed to the rule of law, in our own land and around the world. We believe more than ever in the rights of man, all men of every color, in our own land and around the world. And more than ever we support the United Nations as the best instrument yet devised to promote the peace of the world and to promote the well-being of mankind.

I can tell you today, as I told you in 1958 when I came as majority leader of the United States Senate to the First Committee of this great tribunal, that the full power and partnership of the United States is committed to our joint effort to eliminate war and the threat of war, aggression, and the danger of violence, and to lift from all people everywhere the blight of disease, and poverty, and illiteracy.

Like all human institutions, the United Nations has not achieved the highest of hopes that some held at its birth. Our understanding of how to live, live with one another, is still far behind our knowledge of how to destroy one another.

But as our problems have grown, this organization has grown, in numbers, in authority, in prestige, and its member nations have grown with it, in responsibility and in maturity.

We have seen too much success to become obsessed with failure. The peace-keeping machinery of the United Nations has worked in the Congo, in the

Middle East, and elsewhere. The great transition from colonial rule to independence has been largely accomplished. The decade of development has successfully begun. The world arms race has been slowed. The struggle for human rights has been gaining new force.

And a start has been made in furthering mankind's common interest in outer space, in scientific exploration, in communications, in weather forecasting, in banning the stationing of nuclear weapons, and in establishing principles of law.

I know that vast problems remain, conflicts between great powers, conflicts between small neighbors, disagreements over disarmament, persistence of ancient wrongs in the area of human rights, residual problems of colonialism, and all the rest. But men and nations working apart created these problems, and men and nations working together must solve them.

They can solve them with the help of this organization, when all members make it a workshop for constructive action, and not a forum for abuse; when all members seek its help in settling their own disputes as well as the disputes of others; when all members meet their financial obligations to it; and when all members recognize that no nation and no party and no single system can control the future of man.

A Time for Action

When I entered the Congress of the United States twenty-seven years ago, it was my very great privilege to work closely with President Franklin Delano Roosevelt. As a member of Congress, I worked with him to bring about a profound but peaceful revolution. That peaceful revolution brought help and hope to the one-third of our nation that was then "ill-housed, ill-clad, and ill-nourished."

We helped our working men and women obtain more jobs and we helped them obtain better wages. We helped our farmers to own and improve their own land, and conserve their soil and water, and electrify their farms.

We harnessed the powers of the great rivers, as in the Tennessee Valley and Lower Colorado. We encouraged the growth of cooperatives and trade unions. We curbed the excesses of private speculation. We built homes in the place of city slums, and we extended the rights of freedom of all our citizens.

Now, on the world scale, the time has come, as it came to America thirty years ago, for a new era of hope, hope and progress for that one-third of mankind that is still beset by hunger, poverty, and disease.

In my travels on behalf of my country and President Kennedy, I have seen too much of misery and despair in Africa, in Asia, in Latin America. I have seen too often the ravages of hunger and tapeworm and tuberculosis, and the scabs and scars on too many children who have too little health and no hope.

I think that you and I and our countries and this organization can, and must, do something about these conditions. I am not speaking here of a new way of life to be imposed by any single nation. I am speaking of a higher standard of living, to be inspired by these United Nations. It will not be achieved through some hopeful resolution in this Assembly, but through a peaceful revolution in the world, through a recommitment of all our members, rich and poor, and strong and weak, whatever their location or their ideology, to the basic principles of human welfare and of human dignity.

In this effort, the United States will do its full share. In addition to bilateral aid, we have with great satisfaction assisted in recent years in the emergence and the improvement of international developmental institutions, both within and without this organization.

We favor the steady improvement of collective machinery for helping the less-developed nations build modern societies. We favor an international aid program that is international in practice as well as purpose. Every nation must do its share. All United Nations and their members can do better.

We can act more often together. We can build together a much better world.

The greatest of human problems, and the greatest of our common tasks, is to keep the peace and save the future. All that we have built in the wealth of nations, and all that we plan to do toward a better life for all, will be in vain if our feet should slip, or our vision falter, and our hopes ended in another worldwide war. If there is one commitment more than any other that I would like to leave with you today, it is my unswerving commitment to the keeping and to the strengthening of the peace. Peace is a journey of a thousand miles, and it must be taken one step at a time.

We know what we want: The United States wants to see the cold war end, we want to see it end once and for all; the United States wants to prevent the dissemination of nuclear weapons to nations not now possessing them; the United States wants to press on with arms control and reduction; the United States wants to cooperate with all the members of this organization to conquer everywhere the ancient enemies of mankind—hunger and disease and ignorance; the United States wants sanity, and security, and peace for all, and above all.

President Kennedy, I am sure, would regard as his best memorial the fact that in his three years as

President the world became a little safer and the way ahead became a little brighter. To the protection and the enlargement of this new hope for peace, I pledge my country and its government.

My friends and fellow citizens of the world, soon you will return to your homelands. I hope you will take with you my gratitude for your generosity in hearing me so late in the session. I hope you will convey to your countrymen the gratitude of all Americans for the companionship of sorrow which you shared with us in your messages of the last few weeks. And I hope that you will tell them that the United States of America, sobered by tragedy, united in sorrow, renewed in spirit, faces the New Year determined that world peace, civil rights, and human welfare become not an illusion, but a reality.

Man's age-old hopes remain our goal: that this world, under God, can be safe for diversity, and free from hostility, and a better place for our children and for all generations in the years to come. And therefore, any man and any nation that seeks peace, and hates war, and is willing to fight the good fight against hunger and disease and ignorance and misery, will find the United States of America by their side, willing to walk with them, walk with them every step of the way.

Thank you very much.

_____

I will be brief, for our time is necessarily short and
our agenda is already long.

Last year's Congressional session was the long-
est in peacetime history. And, with that foundation,
let us work together to make this year's session the
best in the nation's history.

Let this session of Congress be known as the session which did more for civil rights than the last
hundred sessions combined; as the session which
enacted the most far-reaching tax cut of our time;
as the session which declared all-out war on human
poverty and unemployment in these United States;
as the session which finally recognized the health
needs of all of our older citizens; as the session
which reformed our tangled transportation and
transit policies; as the session which achieved the
most effective, efficient foreign aid program ever;
and as the session which helped to build more homes
and more schools and more libraries and more hos-

pitals than any single session of Congress in the history of our Republic.

All this and more can and must be done. It can be done by this summer. And it can be done without any increase in spending. In fact, under the budget that I shall shortly submit, it can be done with an actual reduction in federal expenditures and federal employment.

We have in 1964 a unique opportunity and obligation to prove the success of our system, to disprove those cynics and critics at home and abroad who question our purpose and our competence.

If we fail, if we fritter and fumble away our opportunity in needless, senseless quarrels between Democrats and Republicans, or between the House and the Senate, or between the South and the North, or between the Congress and the Administration, then history will rightly judge us harshly.

But if we succeed, if we can achieve these goals by forging in this country a greater sense of union, then, and only then, can we take full satisfaction in the state of the Union.

Here in the Congress you can demonstrate effective legislative leadership by discharging the public business with clarity and dispatch, voting each important proposal up or voting it down, but at least bringing it to a fair and a final vote.

Let us carry forward the plans and programs of

John Fitzgerald Kennedy, not because of our sorrow or sympathy, but because they are right.

And in his memory today, I especially ask all members of my own political faith, in this election year, to put your country ahead of your party and to always debate principles; never debate personalities.

For my part, I pledge a progressive administration which is efficient and honest and frugal.

The budget to be submitted to the Congress shortly is in full accord with this pledge.

It will cut our deficit in half, from $10 billion to $4.9 billion.

It will be, in proportion to our national output, the smallest budget since 19 and 51.

It will call for a substantial reduction in federal employment, a feat accomplished only once before in the last ten years.

While maintaining the full strength of our combat defenses, it will call for the lowest number of civilian personnel in the Department of Defense since 19 and 50.

It will call for total expenditures of $97.9 billion, compared to $98.4 for the current year, a reduction of more than $500 million.

It will call for new obligation authority of $103.8 billion, a reduction of more than $4 billion below last year's request of $107.9 billion.

But it is not a stand-still budget, for America cannot afford to stand still. Our population is growing. Our economy is more complex. Our people's needs are expanding.

But by closing down obsolete installations, by curtailing less urgent programs, by cutting back where cutting back seems to be wise, by insisting on a dollar's worth for a dollar spent, I am able to recommend in this reduced budget the most federal support in history for education, for health, for retraining the unemployed, and for helping the economically and the physically handicapped.

This budget, and this year's legislative program, are designed to help each and every American citizen fulfill his basic hopes:

His hopes for a fair chance to make good.

His hopes for fair play from the law.

His hopes for a full-time job on full-time pay.

His hopes for a decent home for his family in a decent community.

His hopes for a good school for his children with good teachers.

And his hopes for security when faced with sickness or unemployment or old age.

Unfortunately, many Americans live on the outskirts of hope, some because of their poverty and some because of their color, and all too many because of both.

A Time for Action

We must enact youth employment legislation to put jobless, aimless, hopeless youngsters to work on useful projects.

We must distribute more food to the needy through a broader food stamp program.

We must create a National Service Corps to help the economically handicapped of our own country, as the Peace Corps now helps those abroad.

We must modernize our unemployment insurance and establish a high-level commission on automation. If we have the brain power to invent these machines, we have the brain power to make certain that they are a boon and not a bane to humanity.

We must extend the coverage of our minimum wage laws to more than two million workers now lacking this basic protection of purchasing power.

We must, by including special school aid funds as part of our education program, improve the quality of teaching and training and counseling in our hardest-hit areas.

We must build more libraries in every area, and more hospitals and nursing homes under the Hill-Burton Act, and train more nurses to staff them.

We must provide hospital insurance for our older citizens, financed by every worker and his employer under Social Security contributing no more than $1 a month during the employee's working career to protect him in his old age in a dignified manner, without cost to the Treasury, against the devastating hardship of prolonged or repeated illness.

We must, as a part of a revised housing and urban renewal program, give more help to those displaced by slum clearance, provide more housing for our poor and our elderly, and seek as our ultimate goal in our free enterprise system a decent home for every American family.

We must help obtain more modern mass transit within our communities as well as low-cost transportation between them.

Above all, we must release $11 billion of tax reduction into the private spending stream to create new jobs and new markets in every area of this land.

These programs are obviously not for the poor or the underprivileged alone.

Every American will benefit by the extension of Social Security to cover the hospital costs of their aged parents.

Every American community will benefit from the construction or modernization of schools and libraries and hospitals and nursing homes, from the training of more nurses, and from the improvement of urban renewal and public transit.

And every individual American taxpayer, and every corporate taxpayer, will benefit from the earliest possible passage of the pending tax bill, from both the new investment it will bring and the new jobs that it will create.

That tax bill has been thoroughly discussed for a year. Now we need action.

The new budget clearly allows it.

Our taxpayers surely deserve it.

Our economy strongly demands it.

And every month of delay dilutes its benefits in 19 and 64 for consumption, for investment, and for employment.

For until the bill is signed, its investments incentives cannot be deemed certain, and the withholding rate cannot be reduced.

And the most damaging and devastating thing you can do to any businessman in America is to keep him in doubt, and to keep him guessing, on what our tax policy is.

And I say that we should now reduce to 14 per cent, instead of 15 per cent, our withholding rate. And I therefore urge the Congress to take final action on this bill by the first of February, if at all possible.

For, however proud we may be of the unprecedented progress of our free enterprise economy over the last three years, we should not, and we cannot, permit it to pause.

In 1963, for the first time in history, we crossed

the seventy-million job mark, but we will soon need more than seventy-five million jobs.

In 1963, our gross national product reached the $600 billion level, $100 billion higher than when we took office. But it easily could, and it should, be still $30 billion higher today than it is.

Wages and profits and family income are also at their highest level in history, but I would remind you that four million workers and 13 per cent of our industrial capacity are still idle today.

We need a tax cut now to keep this country moving.

For our goal is not merely to spread the work. Our goal is to create more jobs.

I believe the enactment of a thirty-five-hour week would sharply increase costs, would invite inflation, would impair our ability to compete and merely share instead of creating employment.

But I am equally opposed to the forty-five or fifty-hour week in those industries where consistently excessive use of overtime causes increased unemployment.

So, therefore, I recommend legislation authorizing the creation of a tripartite industry committee to determine on an industry-by-industry basis as to where a higher penalty rate for overtime would increase job openings without unduly increasing costs, and authorizing the establishment of such higher rates.

Let me make one principle of this Administration abundantly clear. All of these increased opportunities in employment and education, in housing and in every field must be open to Americans of every color. As far as the writ of federal law will run, we must abolish not some, but all, racial discrimination. For this is not merely an economic issue, or a social, political, or international issue. It is a moral issue, and it must be met by the passage this session of the bill now pending in the House.

All members of the public should have equal access to facilities open to the public.

All members of the public should be equally eligible for federal benefits that are financed by the public.

All members of the public should have an equal chance to vote for public officials and to send their children to good public schools, and to contribute their talents to the public good.

Today Americans of all races stand side by side in Berlin and in Vietnam. They died side by side in Korea. Surely they can work and eat and travel side by side in their own country.

We must also lift by legislation the bars of discrimination against those who seek entry into our country, particularly those with much-needed skills and those joining their families. In establishing preferences, a nation that was built by the immigrants of all lands can ask those who now seek admission: What can you do for our country? But we should not be asking: In what country were you born?

For our ultimate goal is a world without war. A world made safe for diversity, in which all men, goods, and ideas can freely move across every border and every boundary.

We must advance toward this goal in 1964 in at least ten different ways, not as partisans but as patriots.

First, we must maintain—and our reduced defense budget will maintain—that margin of military safety and superiority obtained through three years of steadily increasing both the quality and the quantity of our strategic, our conventional, and our anti-guerrilla forces.

In 1964 we will be better prepared than ever before to defend the cause of freedom, whether it is threatened by outright aggression or by the infiltration practiced by those in Hanoi and Havana who ship arms and men across international borders to foment insurrection.

And we must continue to use that strength, as John Kennedy used it in the Cuban crisis and for the test ban treaty, to demonstrate both the futility of nuclear war and the possibilities of lasting peace.

Second, we must take new steps—and we shall make new proposals at Geneva—toward the control and the eventual abolition of arms. Even in the absence of agreement, we must not stockpile arms beyond our needs, or seek an excess of military power that could be provocative as well as wasteful.

And it is in this spirit that in this fiscal year we are cutting back our production of enriched uranium by 25 per cent; we are shutting down four plutonium piles; we are closing many nonessential military installations. And it is in this spirit that we today call on our adversaries to do the same.

Third, we must make increased use of our food as an instrument of peace, making it available by sale or trade or loan or donation to hungry people in all nations which tell us of their needs and accept proper conditions of distribution.

Fourth, we must assure our pre-eminence in the peaceful exploration of outer space, focusing on an expedition to the moon in this decade, in cooperation with other powers if possible, alone if necessary.

Fifth, we must expand world trade. Having recognized, in the act of 1962, that we must buy as well as sell, we now expect our trading partners to recognize that we must sell as well as buy. We are willing to give them competitive access to our market, asking only that they do the same for us.

Sixth, we must continue, through such measures as the interest equalization tax as well as the co-operation of other nations, our recent progress toward balancing our international accounts. This Administration must and will preserve the present gold value of the dollar.

Seventh, we must become better neighbors with the free states of the Americas, working with the councils of the OAS, with a stronger Alliance for Progress, and with all the men and women of this hemisphere who really believe in liberty and justice for all.

Eighth, we must strengthen the ability of free nations everywhere to develop their independence and raise their standards of living and thereby frustrate those who prey on poverty and chaos. To do this, the rich must help the poor and we must do our part. We must achieve a more rigorous administration of our development assistance, with larger roles for private investors, for other industrialized nations and for international agencies and for the recipient nations themselves.

Ninth, we must strengthen our Atlantic and Pacific partnerships, maintain our alliances, and make the United Nations a more effective instrument for national independence and international order.

Tenth, and finally, we must develop with our allies new means of bridging the gap between the East and the West, facing dangers boldly wherever danger exists, but being equally bold in our search for new agreements which can enlarge the hopes of all while violating the interests of none.

In short, I would say to the Congress that we must be constantly prepared for the worst and constantly acting for the best.

We must be strong enough to win any war and we must be wise enough to prevent one.

We shall neither act as aggressors nor tolerate acts of aggression.

We intend to bury no one, and we do not intend to be buried.

We can fight, if we must, as we have fought before, but we pray that we will never have to fight again.

My good friends and my fellow Americans, in these last sorrowful weeks we have learned anew that nothing is so enduring as faith and nothing is so degrading as hate.

John Kennedy was a victim of hate, but he was also a great builder of faith—faith in our fellow Americans, whatever their creed or their color or their station in life; faith in the future of man, whatever his divisions and differences.

This faith was echoed in all parts of the world. On every continent and in every land to which Mrs. Johnson and I traveled, we found faith and hope and love toward this land of America and toward our people.

So I ask you now, in the Congress and in the country, to join with me in expressing and fulfilling that faith, in working for a nation—a nation that is free from want, and a world that is free from hate; a world of peace and justice and freedom and abundance for our time and for all time to come.

LYNDON B. JOHNSON

President Lyndon B. Johnson was born on August 27, 1908, at Stonewall, Texas. He holds a Bachelor of Science degree from Southwest Texas Teachers College in San Marcos, Texas, and he attended Georgetown Law School in Washington, D.C. in 1935. Sixteen colleges and universities have given him honorary degrees. Mr. Johnson, after teaching school, entered public life in the early 1930's. Before his election to the 75th Congress in 1937, he served as State Director of the National Youth Administration in Texas. In 1948, during his sixth term in the House, he was elected Senator from Texas. Mr. Johnson served in the halls of Congress for twenty-five years, leading his colleagues in the Senate from 1953 until he took the oath as Vice President on January 20, 1961. As Vice President Mr. Johnson was active in the deliberations of the National Security Council and was Chairman of the National Aeronautics and Space Council, of the Peace Corps Advisory Council, of the President's Committee on Equal Employment Opportunity and of the Middle Level Manpower Conference in Puerto Rico. His assignments as Vice President took him to twenty-seven foreign countries. Lyndon B. Johnson took the oath as President of the United States on November 22, 1963.

INDEX

INDEX